Merry Christm

Love,
Joyce

(see p. 78 & 169)

This Place Called Home
A KANSAS CITY
COOKBOOK

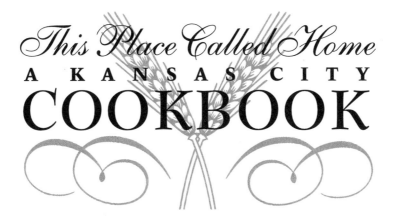

This Place Called Home
A KANSAS CITY
COOKBOOK

Dee Danner Barwick and Judith Fertig

Copyright © 1998 by KCPT Public Television 19
Kansas City, Missouri, 64108

Editors: Dee Barwick and Judith Fertig
Cover design: Jim Langford
Cover photographs: © MIDWESTOCK/© Ron Anderson,
©Bruce Mathews, ©David Morris, ©Kevin Sink, ©Ben Weddle
Text design: Linda Ray, Family Features
Creative direction & production: Options Publishing Co.
Printed in the United States of America
ISBN 1-892431-19-X

Cover photographs: Front cover: 47th & Broadway Fountain, Kevin Sink;
Apple Pie, Ron Anderson; Truman Home, Bruce Mathews; Westport Wagon,
Bruce Mathews; Liberty Memorial, Kevin Sink; BBQ Ribs, David Morris;
Plaza Clock Tower, Bruce Mathews; Bartle Hall, Bruce Mathews. Back cover:
Plaza Sidewalk Cafe, Kevin Sink; Loose Park, Bruce Mathews; Chiefs at Play,
Ben Weddle; Scout & Downtown, Kevin Sink; Shuttlecock at Nelson, Bruce
Mathews; Meyer Circle Fountain, Kevin Sink; Kauffman Stadium, Bruce
Mathews; 47th & Broadway Fountain, Bruce Mathews.
Interior photographs: page 1, Kevin Sink; page 21, Bruce Mathews; page 37,
Bruce Mathews; page 55, David Morris; page 95, Bruce Mathews; page 125,
Kevin Sink; page 141, Ron Anderson.

Additional copies of *This Place Called Home, A Kansas City Cookbook* may
be obtained by using the order form at back of book
or by calling (816) 756-3580, extension 4244, or by contacting:
Cookbook Sales
KCPT – Channel 19
125 East 31st Street
Kansas City, Missouri 64108

To order by email: cookbook@kcpt.org

PUBLIC TELEVISION 19

ACKNOWLEDGMENTS

First and foremost, thanks go to the many talented cooks of the Kansas City area who shared their recipes and made this book possible. For reasons of space not all recipes could be included but the review of them dictated the balance and content of the book and helped the editors put together a representative collection of how we cook in the Heartland. (A complete list of contributors whose recipes appear in the book can be found on page 175.)

Sincere appreciation to Susan Anderson of **MIDWESTOCK** and photographers Ron Anderson, Bruce Mathews, David Morris, Kevin Sink and Ben Weddle for donating the rights to use the photographs which appear on the cover and throughout the book. And a special thanks to Susan Anderson, who also spent time researching, recommending and organizing the photographs.

A collection such as this requires the efforts of many. Bravo to Joy Hesler, Linda Hill, Joyce Kemp, Warren Maus, Lois Martin, Deanne Pearson, Kaleen Tiber, Ann Docherty, Mary Ann Duckers, David Hogerty, Millie Krna, Karen Adler, Sally Buck and the staff of Walsworth Printing. They've reviewed, revised, advised, encouraged, organized, tested, tasted, written, rewritten, proofread and woven together the many tasks and details that make a book "happen." Special thanks to JoAnne Owens who prepared all copy for the typesetters and made valuable editorial suggestions, to Linda Ray and Jeff Fetrow of Family Features for typesetting and design consultation, and to Jim Langford who created a great cover!

Dedicated to the members and supporters of KCPT Public Television 19.

CONTENTS

INTRODUCTION

Since its establishment as a community-licensed public television station in 1972, KCPT Public Television 19 has enjoyed being an active part of the Kansas City community. KCPT's insightful programming has enriched many lives with hours of uninterrupted, quality, informational entertainment. And in the changing world of digital technologies, KCPT has expanded its offerings to include a variety of telecommunications services—from an award-winning Internet home page to interactive on-line offerings for parents and teachers.

Along the way, KCPT has introduced Kansas City to a broad range of personalities—from Fred Rogers to Jim Lehrer, from Elmo to Arthur, from Pavarotti to Jacques Pepin. Together, KCPT and Kansas City have journeyed to the moon, explored endangered coral reefs, felt the heartbreak and frustration of lost love, and come to better understand the miracles of life, nature and the universe. Every day KCPT is invited into homes as a welcome guest and guide to expanded knowledge, richer understanding and quality experiences.

Just as the community has embraced KCPT, KCPT has come to know and appreciate its viewers and its community. Kansas City is a rich and varied place with a cultural heritage that flavors its customs and its cuisines. Where else can you dine on the best in grain-fed beef one night, melt-in-your-mouth Choucroute Garni the next, and Savory Lebanese Meat Pies the next? Kansas City is a place where east meets west, north meets south and everything is blended into a unique and satisfying place to call home.

And from this place in the nation's heartland, everyone knows that wheat fields and bountiful farms are just beyond even the most urban horizon. Such a perspective, when paired with a diverse cultural heritage, means food is real here—it is something to be savored, enjoyed and shared with friends and family.

That's why KCPT has chosen to publish *This Place Called Home, A Kansas City Cookbook.* Food is often what helps define a culture and a community. This cookbook, with its variety of offerings reflects the simple suppers, special dishes and delectable desserts that fuel our every day lives. These are real recipes from real people in the KCPT community—and they reflect the kinds of foods to be found on plates at potlucks, in cookie jars on kitchen counters, and at the center of family gatherings and memories.

Sit down, relax, and experience a "taste" of Kansas City—a place KCPT is proud to call home.

Mission Statement of KCPT Public Television 19

To use the power of telecommunications
to enrich people's lives.

Visit KCPT's web site.
www.kcpt.org

Appetizers & Snacks

When Kansas Citians gather for a festive event, you know there will be good food. Small savory bites paired with favorite beverages start any gathering on a convivial note. Inspired by cooking shows, travels to foreign lands and great produce from local markets, Kansas Citians have created a delectable array of appetizers. Bon Appetit!

Kansas City Barbecued Brisket Dip

Almond Dip

Cucumber Dip

Curried Vegetable Dip

Pecan Crusted Artichoke Dip

Farmers' Market Eggplant Spread

Roasted Pepper, Tomato and Cheese

Savory Bacon Cheddar Cheesecake

Thai Peanut Sauce

Chicken Saté

Smoked Salmon Paté

Peach Quesadillas

Sassy Salsa Squares

Artichoke Feta Tortilla Wraps

Chez Les Canses French KC Wrap

Easy Spanokopita

Stromboli

Mini Potato Latkes

...and more!

KANSAS CITY BARBECUED BRISKET DIP

1 pound chopped barbecued brisket
1/2 cup chopped onion
1 clove garlic, minced
1 1/4 cups barbecue sauce
1 (4-ounce) can chopped jalapeno peppers, drained
1 (8-ounce) package cream cheese, softened
1/3 cup grated pecorino (sheep milk cheese), monterey
  jack or parmesan

Combine all ingredients and bake at 350 degrees in a ceramic baking dish 20 to 30 minutes, or until heated through. Serve with French bread. Makes 8 to 10 servings.

ALMOND DIP

1 1/2 cups sour cream
1/2 cup ground almonds
Juice and grated zest of 1 lemon
Kosher salt and freshly ground black pepper to taste

Mix sour cream, almonds, juice and zest together in a small bowl. Taste, then add salt and pepper as needed. Makes 2 cups.

"This dip recipe is one I put together after tasting a similar one while on vacation in Sedona."
Ardie Davis aka Remus Powers, Ph.B.(Doctor of Barbecue Philosophy) Mission, Kansas

Barbara Reed, Shawnee Mission, Kansas, likes to serve this dip in a hollowed-out green cabbage, surrounded by small red radishes, pencil-thin asparagus, and haricots vert (very thin French green beans).

CUCUMBER DIP

1 large cucumber, peeled and shredded
1 (8-ounce) package cream cheese, softened
1 tablespoon mayonnaise
2 dashes red pepper sauce
1 dash worcestershire Sauce
Minced garlic to taste
Minced onion to taste

Pat the shredded cucumber dry between 2 layers of paper towels and set aside. Beat cream cheese and mayonnaise together until fluffy. Add cucumbers and all seasonings to cheese mixture and stir well to blend. Cover and refrigerate for at least one hour before serving. Makes 1 1/2 cups.

"A bridge-playing friend gave me this recipe many years ago. Back then we enjoyed it with potato chips—now I serve with pretzels, crackers or a tray of raw vegetables."
Carlene Pasche
Overland Park, Kansas

CURRY DIP

1/2 cup mayonnaise
1/2 cup sour cream
1 heaping teaspoon horseradish
1 heaping teaspoon curry powder
1 teaspoon minced onion
1 teaspoon garlic salt
1 tablespoon vinegar
1 tablespoon sugar

In a small bowl combine all ingredients; stir to mix well. Makes 1 cup.

"This is a dip I make often—it's good and easy. It's best when made the day before you plan to serve it."
Pat Wright
Lee's Summit, Missouri

CURRIED VEGETABLE DIP

1 rib celery
1 carrot, peeled
1 small onion
2 plum tomatoes, peeled
2 tablespoons butter
1 tablespoon curry powder
1/2 cup sour cream
4 ounces cream cheese, softened
Lemon juice, cracked black pepper, and kosher salt to taste

In a food processor finely chop the celery, carrot, onion and tomatoes. Melt butter in a saucepan and sauté the chopped vegetables until their moisture has evaporated. Add the curry powder and sauté for another 2 to 3 minutes. Let cool, then use a fork to mix vegetables with sour cream and cream cheese. Add lemon juice, pepper and salt to taste. Makes 2 cups.

KCPT *ip: Make a low-fat version of this dip by using low fat sour cream and cream cheese.*

Sara and Bill Morgan, Kansas City, Missouri, love to entertain. Their busy schedules dictate that the menu be simple, yet sophisticated. This recipe is a delicious example of both qualities. They serve it with fresh vegetables and pita bread or French bread toasts.

PECAN CRUSTED ARTICHOKE DIP

"I developed this recipe many years ago and it is always a great hit at parties. Serve with warm pita triangles."
Kathryn Moore
Lee's Summit, Missouri

4 tablespoons butter or margarine, divided
1 medium onion, finely chopped
3 cloves garlic, minced
4 cups coarsely chopped fresh spinach
1 (14-ounce) can artichoke hearts, drained and chopped
1 (8-ounce) package cream cheese, softened and cut into
   1/2-inch cubes
1/2 cup mayonnaise
1/2 cup parmesan cheese
2 cups shredded cheddar cheese
2 dashes hot pepper sauce
2/3 cup chopped pecans

Melt 3 tablespoons butter in large skillet over medium-high heat. Add onion and garlic and cook 3 minutes. Add spinach and cook for 3 to 5 minutes, stirring frequently. Remove from heat. Add artichoke hearts, cream cheese, mayonnaise, parmesan cheese, cheddar cheese and hot sauce to spinach mixture. Stir until well blended. Place in a lightly greased 1 1/2 quart casserole. Melt remaining butter and add pecans; toss until coated; set aside. Bake spinach-artichoke mixture at 350 degrees for 20 minutes. Top with pecans and bake an additional 15 minutes. Makes 15 to 20 appetizer servings.

QUICK ARTICHOKE DIP

Ed Scanlon, Kansas City, Missouri, shared his family cookbook. This quick and easy recipe is from Bridget.

1 cup freshly grated parmesan cheese
1 cup mayonnaise
1 (14-ounce) can artichoke hearts, drained and chopped

Preheat oven to 350 degrees. In a medium bowl combine all ingredients; stir to mix well. Put in a lightly greased 1 1/2 quart baking dish. Bake for 15 to 20 minutes, until lightly browned. Makes 6 to 8 servings.

FARMERS' MARKET EGGPLANT SPREAD

2 large eggplants, stemmed and sliced
1 tablespoon salt
4 large garlic cloves
1 teaspoon dried tarragon
1/4 teaspoon ground black pepper
1 teaspoon sugar
1/2 cup olive oil

Sprinkle salt on both sides of each eggplant slice and lay on paper towels to drain. This removes the eggplant's bitterness. Using an oiled grill basket, grill eggplant over medium coals until softened, about 5 to 7 minutes per side. (Or broil in oven, but grilling gives better flavor!) Place grilled eggplant in food processor or blender; add garlic, tarragon, pepper, and sugar. Purée to a fine paste. With the machine running, drizzle in the olive oil so mixture is of spread consistency. Serve on flat bread or crackers. Makes 8 servings.

KCPT *ip:* *For a special presentation, use any dip or spread to make Stuffed Cherry Tomatoes. Use a mixture of yellow and red cherry tomatoes, if possible. Cut off the stem end and scoop some of the pulp out with a melon baller or grapefruit spoon. Fill the cavity with your favorite dip or spread and dust the top with chopped parsley.*

Kansas Citians love to get up early on summer Saturdays to hit their favorite farmers' markets. Graphic designer Mary Carroll, Kansas City, Missouri, tasted this spread at a farmers' market and fell in love with it. She recreated the appetizer in her own kitchen, and passes this recipe on to lucky us!

ROASTED PEPPER, TOMATO AND CHEESE

Jan Rodgers, Kansas City, Missouri, developed this superb recipe after tasting a similar one at a tiny restaurant in Gordes, France. It has become a favorite of her Cellarmasters group!

2 red bell peppers
2 yellow bell peppers
2 orange bell peppers
6 plum tomatoes
6 ounces goat cheese
6 ounces fromage blanc
salt and pepper to taste
2 tablespoons olive oil
Arugula and basil leaves for garnish

Roast, seed and peel peppers and tomatoes, using oven or grill methods described below. Cool, chop and place in an oiled 9 x 13 baking dish, sprinkle lightly with salt and pepper; set aside. In a medium bowl blend the cheeses together. Top vegetable mixture with spoonfuls of cheese mixture. Drizzle olive oil over all and place under broiler until top is bubbly. Garnish with arugula and basil leaves. Serve with French bread. Makes 10 servings.

KCPT *ip: For easy roasting, preheat oven to 425 degrees. Line a baking sheet with foil. Cut peppers and tomatoes in half; discard stems, membranes and seeds. Cut in half again. Place, cut sides down, on baking sheet. Bake until skins are dark and blistered (but not burnt), about 20 minutes. Remove from sheet and immediately wrap in foil or place in a paper bag. Let sit to "steam" for 30 minutes. This will ensure easy peeling.*

To prepare on an outdoor grill, remove stems and coat outsides with oil. Place on an oiled rack or basket. Grill directly over heat, turning often, until skins are lightly charred, 8 to 10 minutes, depending on intensity of the fire. Wrap in foil or paper bag, let sit for 30 minutes. Then peel, seed and slice or chop.

SAVORY BACON CHEDDAR CHEESECAKE

2 tablespoons margarine
2 tablespoons breadcrumbs
1 pound smoked bacon, chopped
1/2 cup finely chopped onion
8 ounces shredded sharp cheddar cheese
4 (8-ounce) packages cream cheese, cut into pieces, at
   room temperature
5 eggs, beaten
2 tablespoons flour
2 red bell peppers, seeded and diced
1/2 teaspoon black pepper
2 cups chutney, for garnish
Grapes or other fruit, for garnish

Preheat oven to 325 degrees. Grease a 9-inch springform pan with margarine and dust with breadcrumbs. Wrap the outside of the pan with foil. In a large skillet sauté bacon until crisp. Remove the bacon and drain on paper towels. Sauté the onion in the bacon grease until transparent. Using food processor, blend the bacon and onion with the cheddar cheese. Gradually add the cream cheese and eggs. Add the flour, bell pepper and black pepper and blend well. Pour the mixture into the prepared pan and place it in a deep pan with enough water to reach up the sides of the springform pan. Bake for 1 hour or until a knife inserted in the center comes out clean. Cover and chill for several hours before serving. To serve, remove from the pan and place on a cake plate. Spread chutney over top and garnish with grapes or other fruit. Serve at room temperature with crackers. Makes 25 appetizer servings.

Leawood, Kansas resident Rose Kallas likes to make this rich appetizer cheesecake when she's expecting a crowd. "You can make it ahead of time, and it looks great on the buffet table," she says.

TOMATO CAPER CHEESE BALL

Joy Hesler, Shawnee Mission, Kansas, presents this unique cheese ball on a colorful lettuce leaf.

1 (8-ounce) package cream cheese, softened
3 tablespoons butter, softened
1 (4-ounce) package sun-dried tomatoes, finely chopped
2 cloves garlic, minced
2 tablespoons capers

Combine cheese, butter, tomatoes and garlic, mix well and form into ball. Press capers into surface. Chill to blend flavors. Serve at room temperature.

THAI PEANUT SAUCE

Sarah Huntman Reed, of Kansas City, Missouri, calls this her "two-minute sauce" because it's so fast and easy to make. She serves it with Chicken Saté and chilled fresh vegetables or, for a side dish, over cooked Asian noodles.

1 cup roasted, salted Virginia peanuts
5 ounces Asian sweet chili sauce (not garlic style, available at Asian markets)
Juice of half a lime
2 tablespoons hot water

Place peanuts in food processor with steel blade. Cycle on and off until consistency of chunky peanut butter. Take care not to process further. Add chili sauce and lime juice; process a second or two to blend. Add hot water and blend a second more. Makes 1 1/2 cups.

CHICKEN SATÉ

1 pound boneless chicken breast, sliced into long, thin strips
1 cup teriyaki marinade

Marinate chicken in teriyaki for 1 hour. Soak 12 to 16 wooden skewers in water for at least 30 minutes. Build a fire in the grill. Thread each piece of chicken onto a skewer and grill on both sides until done, about 5 minutes. Serve with Thai Peanut Sauce for dipping. Makes 4 servings.

CHICKEN PATÉ

1/4 cup (1/2 stick) butter
1 medium onion, chopped
3 whole chicken breasts, boned, skinned and cut into
  small pieces
1 cup tawny port wine, divided
1 (3-ounce) package cream cheese, softened
2 tablespoons heavy cream
1 1/4 teaspoon dry tarragon, crumbled
1 teaspoon salt or to taste
1/4 teaspoon pepper or to taste
1 (2 3/4-ounce) package slivered almonds, toasted
Paprika

Melt butter in skillet. Add onion and chicken. Sauté over moderate heat for about 8 minutes. Add 1/2 cup wine and bring to a boil. Cook over medium heat until liquid is reduced to about half. Transfer mixture to blender or food processor; purée. Add cheese, cream, tarragon, salt, pepper and remaining wine. Process until smooth. Add almonds, mixing by hand and reserving some almonds for garnish. Pack paté firmly into stoneware crock, cover tightly and refrigerate for 1 to 2 days before serving. To serve, sprinkle paprika on top and garnish with reserved almonds. Makes 4 cups.

Gary Jensen, Kansas City, Missouri, won a prize for this tasty paté recipe which is ideal as part of a festive buffet.

SMOKED SALMON PATÉ

Mary Pfeifer Langley, of Kansas City, Missouri, serves this paté on party pumpernickel bread, topped with a sprinkle of dill.

2/3 cup chopped smoked salmon
1 cup heavy cream
2 teaspoons lemon juice
3 teaspoons capers
1/4 teaspoon dill
Pepper to taste

Place all ingredients in food processor or blender; blend until combined. Cover and refrigerate for at least 3 hours before serving. Makes 1 2/3 cups.

PEACH QUESADILLAS

"I always use no-fat cream cheese—tastes great and makes me feel virtuous. I've also made this recipe with fresh mangos and papayas."
Joy Hesler
Shawnee Mission, Kansas

4 ounces cream cheese
8 flour tortillas
1 fresh Anaheim chili, chopped
2 fresh peaches, peeled and sliced (about 1 1/2 cups)

Spread cream cheese on four of the tortillas. Add chili and fruit. Top with remaining tortillas. Cook in a dry skillet over medium heat, until lightly browned on both sides, about 2 to 3 minutes. Cut into wedges to serve.

SASSY SALSA SQUARES

Best if made on day it's to be served—serve at room temperature.

2 cups shredded cheddar cheese
2 cups shredded Monterey Jack cheese
1/2 cup salsa
3 eggs, beaten

Combine cheeses. Mix salsa and eggs together. In a 9-inch square baking dish, layer half the cheese mixture, add all of salsa mixture, top with remaining cheese. Bake 30 minutes at 350 degrees. Cool before cutting into one-inch squares.

ARTICHOKE FETA (NEVER HAD BETTAH) TORTILLA WRAPS

1 (14-ounce) can artichoke hearts, rinsed, drained, and
  finely chopped
3 green onions, thinly sliced
3 tablespoons prepared pesto
1/4 cup feta cheese, crumbled
2 tablespoons grated parmesan cheese
2 tablespoons grated romano cheese
8 (8-inch) flour tortillas
8 cherry tomatoes, sliced into halves, for garnish
1 cup plain yogurt, for garnish
Cilantro leaves, for garnish

Preheat oven to 350 degrees. Combine artichoke hearts, green onion, pesto, and cheeses. Place 1/4 cup of mixture in center of each tortilla. Roll up tortillas, securing with toothpicks. Arrange in 3-quart rectangular baking dish. Bake uncovered for 20 to 25 minutes. To serve, attach 1 tomato half to each toothpick; top with yogurt and cilantro leaves. Makes 8 servings.

"I created this recipe and my son Michael named it. This recipe was just one of the things we shared—he introduced our family to pesto, feta cheese and other wonderful foods. As a free lance writer, I find that creating a recipe is a lot like writing a short story."
Judith Bader Jones
Fairway, Kansas

Kansas Citians have long appreciated the portable sandwich—whether it was a fried Cheese Frenchie or burnt ends on a bun. Today, the sandwich of choice is the wrap. For tailgate picnics, a school lunch or a snack with friends, these wraps pack a lot of flavor into small packages.

BARBECUED BEEF WRAP

**1 large lavosh flatbread, moistened between two tea
   towels**
1 cup black bean dip
1 pound burnt ends or brisket, shredded
1/4 cup chopped fresh cilantro
1 cup barbecue sauce for dipping

Place the softened lavosh on a flat surface. Spread the black bean dip over it leaving a 1-inch margin all around. Top with meat, sprinkle cilantro on meat and roll up jellyroll style. Wrap in foil until ready to serve. To serve, slice the wrap into 1 1/2-inch slices and arrange on a serving platter. Offer barbecue sauce as a dip. Makes 6 servings.

"CHEZ LES CANSES" FRENCH KC WRAP

2 cloves garlic, minced
1 cup mayonnaise
6 large flour tortillas
1 (8-ounce) jar roasted red peppers or pimentos, drained
1/4 cup chopped fresh watercress or parsley
1 pound grilled pork tenderloin, sliced into thin strips

Combine garlic with mayonnaise and spread mixture on tortillas leaving a 1-inch margin around the sides. Spread peppers over mayonnaise, then top with watercress or parsley. Top with pork slices. Fold top and bottom edges of each tortilla over the filling, then roll lengthwise in jelly roll fashion. Wrap in foil and chill until ready to serve. Makes 6 servings.

FAST AND FABULOUS FILLED FOCCACIA

1 (10-inch) loaf foccacia
1/2 to 1 cup herbed cream cheese spread
1 cup spinach leaves
1/2 cup thinly sliced red onion
1 red bell pepper, seeded and sliced
1/4 to 1/2 cup Italian salad dressing
1/2 cup bean sprouts
6 to 8 slices provolone cheese

Slice foccacia in half horizontally. Spread bottom layer with cream cheese. Cover with spinach leaves. Add onion and pepper. Pour on salad dressing. Add thin layer of bean sprouts. Top with slices of Provolone cheese, overlapping to cover. Place top half of foccacia on cheese. Wrap in foil and heat in 325 degree oven for 15 to 20 minutes. Cut in wedges. Makes 6 to 8 servings.

KEPTip: *For a brunch dish, fill foccacia with cooked scrambled eggs, diced ham or sausage and thinly sliced onions and peppers. Top with shredded or sliced cheddar cheese. Wrap in foil and heat until warmed through.*

Terry Cooper of Fairway, Kansas, enjoys entertaining. This easy appetizer is a favorite of his guests. It also makes a wonderful light lunch—serve with a bowl of fresh fruit salad. Terry also prepares a "Greek" version by using basil-flavored cream cheese, black olives, sun-dried tomatoes and feta cheese.

EASY SPANAKOPITA

4 egg whites, divided
**2 (10-ounce) packages frozen chopped spinach, thawed
   and well drained**
12 ounces small curd cottage cheese, drained
6 ounces feta cheese
1 1/2 tablespoons chopped fresh dill
2 (8-ounce) packages refrigerated crescent dinner rolls

Preheat oven to 400 degrees. In a large bowl, combine 3 egg whites, spinach, cheeses, and dill; set aside. Unroll one can of the rolls and separate into 2 large rectangles. Place in the bottom of a 13 x 9 baking pan. Bake for 5 minutes. Spread spinach-cheese mixture evenly over the baked crust. Unroll second can of rolls, separate into two rectangles to form top crust, stretching to cover filling completely. Beat remaining egg white until frothy and brush over top crust. Bake for 30 to 40 minutes, covering with foil halfway through baking if crust is browning too early. Makes 10 to 12 servings.

STROMBOLI

1 (1-pound) loaf frozen bread dough
1/2 pound bulk Italian sausage
1 egg
2 tablespoon olive oil, divided
Italian seasoning to taste
Black pepper to taste
1 (4-ounce) package sliced pepperoni
1/2 pound deli ham, shaved and shredded
1/2 pound mozzarella, shredded

Thaw bread dough according to package directions. Brown sausage and put aside. Roll dough into a 16" x 8" rectangle. Beat egg with 1 tablespoon oil and spread evenly over the dough. Sprinkle with Italian seasonings and pepper. Arrange pepperoni over the dough, then cover with ham and sausage. Top with cheese. Roll as you would for a jelly roll, starting with the long side. Seal the edge and ends. Brush top and sides with remaining oil. Bake in a 375 degree oven for 20 minutes or until the roll is nicely browned. Let cool for 15 to 20 minutes before slicing into 1" slices. Makes 12 to 16 servings.

KCPT *ip: Make a vegetarian version by substituting about 2 cups of sautéed vegetables (any combination of broccoli, cauliflower, carrots, mushrooms, zucchini, onions, etc.) for the meats. Be sure to sauté the veggies until they are no longer wet. This is key—soggy veggies make a soggy stromboli.*

"For party food I can't recommend anything more popular than this stromboli. Comments range from "What is this?" to "Is there any more?" in record time. There is no such thing as leftover stromboli!"
Kayla Folger
Topeka, Kansas

SAVORY LEBANESE MEAT PIES

1 package of 30 Rhodes frozen white rolls
1 pound ground chuck
1 medium onion, finely chopped
Salt and pepper to taste
1/4 teaspoon allspice
2 tablespoons cream cheese
1/2 cup lemon juice
1/2 cup melted butter

Thaw rolls according to package directions, cut each in half. Cover with cloth and let rise. Brown meat and onions lightly in skillet. Combine meat mixture with spices, cheese and lemon juice. Roll each piece of dough out into a circle. Put 1 tablespoon meat mixture in center. Fold dough over meat into center so it forms a semi-circle. Crimp edges with a fork. Bake at 400 degrees until dough is brown, approximately 13 minutes. Immediately brush pies with melted butter. Makes 60 small pies.

ROASTED NEW POTATOES WITH TAPENADE

3 pounds new potatoes
Olive oil
Garlic salt
1 (12-ounce) jar tapenade
Chopped parsley to garnish

Preheat oven to 350 degrees. Wash and trim potatoes, then rub with olive oil and sprinkle with salt. Place on a baking tray and roast in oven for 30 to 45 minutes, stirring occasionally. Cut each potato in half and trim the bottom so each half will sit upright. Arrange potato halves on serving trays and place a small spoonful of tapenade on each. Sprinkle with parsley and serve. Makes 10 to 12 servings.

MINI POTATO LATKES
WITH SMOKED SALMON AND DILL

1 small onion, grated and sieved to remove extra liquid
2 large baking potatoes, peeled and shredded
2 eggs, beaten
Salt and pepper to taste
2 tablespoons flour
1/4 cup vegetable oil for frying
1/3 cup sour cream
1/4 cup chopped smoked salmon
Fresh dill sprigs

Preheat the oven to 300 degrees. Line a baking sheet with a double thickness of paper towels. Press the shredded potatoes between layers of paper towels to remove extra moisture. Place potatoes and onions in a mixing bowl. Beat in the eggs, seasonings, and flour until batter is stiff. Heat oil in a large frying pan. For each latke, drop 1/2 tablespoon of batter into the hot oil and flatten it with a spatula. Fry for 2 to 3 minutes on one side, then carefully turn and fry for 2 minutes more on the other side, or until golden brown. Transfer the latkes to the paper-lined baking sheet to drain. Place in the oven to keep warm until all are cooked. To serve, arrange the pancakes on a large platter. Garnish each with a dollop of sour cream, a sprinkling of smoked salmon, and a dill sprig. Makes 30 to 36 mini pancakes.

Latkes are a traditional part of Jewish holiday menus. For a side dish they are often served with fresh applesauce.

ST. JOSEPH'S TABLE STUFFED ARTICHOKES

6 fresh artichokes, trimmed
2 teaspoons salt, divided
1 large garlic clove, minced
1/2 cup freshly grated parmesan cheese
1 tablespoon minced Italian parsley
3/4 teaspoon pepper
2 cups fresh bread crumbs
1/2 cup olive oil, divided
1 lemon, cut in half

Trim 1/2 inch off the top of each artichoke, and trim the bottom of each so that it will stand firmly in the pan. Holding each artichoke firmly, strike the bottom down on a table to open the leaves. Put the artichokes in a large pot of cold water, add 1 teaspoon of the salt, and let stand for 20 minutes. Drain well and set aside. Combine the garlic, parmesan, parsley, pepper, and bread crumbs. Add enough olive oil to just moisten. Spread open the artichoke leaves and pack a little of the bread crumb mixture in each leaf. Repeat with each artichoke. Place the stuffed artichokes in a covered casserole dish or large saucepan and fill the pan with about 2 inches of water. Add the remaining 1 teaspoon salt to the water along with the lemon halves. Drizzle the remaining olive oil over artichokes. Cover and cook over medium heat for 1 hour, or until a leaf pulled from an artichoke is tender. Makes 6 servings.

On St. Joseph's Day, March 19, old Sicilian family recipes are made in quantity and shared with the community at several different churches. At Holy Rosary in Columbus Park, everything from pasta con sarde (a meatless sauce) to these savory stuffed artichokes to different kinds of frittatas exemplifies the richness of Sicilian cuisine. Everyone comes away with a bag of biscotti (Italian cookies), and wonderful memories.

Salads

Salad days are any days in Kansas City. That perennial summertime favorite, potato salad, shares space with fresh marinated vegetables and spicy black beans. Pasta salads are a year-round favorite and a tasty plate of pasta often serves as a light meal. Freshly-tossed green salad, dressed with a lively vinaigrette or a creamy cheese dressing, complements the soups and stews of winter. And many a holiday meal has been enhanced by a tempting fruit salad.

Westport Room Salad Dressing

Work-of-Art Vinaigrette

Blue Cheese Dressing

Puckerbrush Road Lettuce Salad

Orange-Avacado Toss

Spinach Salad with Creamy Dressing

Jicama and Red Sweet Pepper Salad

Broccoli Slaw

Red, White and Green Bean Salad

Hominy Salad

Spicy Black Bean Salad with Lime Vinaigrette

Weston Fourth of July Potato Salad

The Best Wurst Potato Salad

Greek Style Couscous Salad

Rotini Nicoise

Saucy Cherry Layered Salad

Frozen Cranberry Salad

...and more!

WESTPORT ROOM SALAD DRESSING

2 cups mayonnaise
2 cloves garlic, minced
6 tablespoons grated parmesan cheese
2 tablespoons lemon juice
1/2 cup non-dairy creamer (mocha-mix)
salt and pepper to taste

In a medium bowl combine all ingredients; whisk well to blend. Chill for 2 to 24 hours before serving. Keeps up to one month in refrigerator. Makes 3 cups.

A KC favorite— this dressing recipe is from the old Westport Room in Union Station where the salad was served topped with grated cauliflower and bread crumbs.

WORK-OF-ART VINAIGRETTE

1 large garlic clove
1 teaspoon fine sea salt
3 tablespoons extra-virgin olive oil
1 tablespoon fresh lemon juice

In a mortar and pestle mash the garlic and salt to a fine paste. Using pestle to stir, blend in the olive oil and lemon juice. Pour the dressing over salad greens for 6 to 8 people; using your clean hands, toss the salad so the dressing leaves a very light coating on the greens. Serve at once.

This recipe came from Mary Langley's friend, Marian Bowie, who once lived in Greece. A restaurateur fell in love with the dressing. In exchange for the recipe, he gave her an oil painting which had hung over his bar for many years! Thus the name.

BLUE CHEESE DRESSING

Rumor has it that Bill Reed is very fond of blue cheese dressing. So this recipe was developed especially for him—a classic dressing at its best. (For Bill, maybe a little extra blue cheese on top!)

4 ounces blue cheese
1 cup mayonnaise
3 tablespoons sour cream
2 teaspoons lemon juice
dash of salt
1 to 2 drops worcestershire sauce
1 to 2 drops hot sauce
1 clove garlic, finely minced, optional

Break cheese into small pieces and set aside. In mixing bowl combine mayonnaise, sour cream, lemon juice, salt, worcestershire sauce, hot sauce and garlic, if desired. Whisk well. Gently stir in cheese; do not overmix. Keep refrigerated. Makes about 1 1/2 cups.

PUCKERBRUSH ROAD LETTUCE SALAD WITH AVOCADO-DILL DRESSING

Sandy Wheeler, Independence, Missouri, loves to entertain, and this salad has graced many a neighborhood party. The dressing doubles as a great dip for vegetables.

Avocado-Dill Dressing
1/2 cup mayonnaise
1/2 cup sour cream
1/4 cup dill pickle juice
1/2 avocado, mashed
1 tablespoon chopped parsley
2 teaspoons chopped chives
1 teaspoon dill weed

1 bunch red leaf lettuce, torn
1 cup sliced fresh mushrooms
1 small Bermuda onion, sliced and separated into rings
1 green pepper, sliced into rings
1/2 medium avocado, peeled and sliced

Combine all dressing ingredients. Chill for at least 1 hour. In large bowl combine lettuce, mushrooms, onion, green pepper and avocado. Refrigerate. Just before serving, toss with dressing. Makes 6 servings.

ORANGE-AVOCADO TOSS
WITH ORANGE VINAIGRETTE

Orange Vinaigrette
1/2 teaspoon grated orange peel
1/4 cup orange juice
1/2 cup salad oil
2 tablespoons sugar
2 tablespoons red wine vinegar
1 tablespoon lemon juice
1/4 teaspoon salt

1 medium head lettuce
1 small cucumber, thinly sliced
1 avocado, seeded, peeled, sliced
1 (11-ounce) can mandarin oranges, drained
2 tablespoons sliced green onions

For the vinaigrette, combine all ingredients in a container with screw-top lid; cover and shake well to blend. Set aside. In a large bowl combine salad ingredients. Just before serving, shake dressing again and pour over salad. Toss lightly.

KCPT *ip: To make a presto salad dressing or vegetable dip, combine half an avocado with 1/2 cup of vinaigrette dressing. Process in blender until smooth.*

This salad, that pleases the eye as well as the palate, comes from Luella Dick of King City, Missouri. To prevent browning of sliced avocados, she suggests brushing surface with lemon juice.

SPINACH SALAD WITH CREAMY DRESSING

Mary Ann Duckers, Prairie Village, Kansas, serves this salad at every special family occasion—and every member of her family expects her to do so!

Creamy Dressing
1 cup oil
5 tablespoons red wine vinegar
4 tablespoons sour cream
2 teaspoons chopped fresh parsley
2 cloves garlic, crushed
1/2 teaspoon dry mustard
2 tablespoons sugar
1 1/2 teaspoon salt
ground pepper to taste

1 1/4 pounds fresh spinach, torn
4 hard boiled eggs, chopped
8 strips bacon, cooked and crumbled

For the dressing, combine all ingredients in container with screw-top lid, cover and shake well to mix. Chill for 6 to 24 hours. When ready to serve, place spinach, eggs and bacon in a large bowl, pour dressing over mixture and toss gently to coat. Makes 8 servings.

POPPY SEED-CHEESE DRESSING

Lynn Sample, Overland Park, Kansas, eliminates the hard boiled eggs from her spinach salad and uses this dressing which she got from her friend Jorine Butterfield Silcox.

1/4 cup sugar
1 teaspoon finely-grated onion
1 cup vegetable oil
1/3 cup cider vinegar
1 teaspoon poppy seeds
1 teaspoon salt
1 teaspoon dry mustard
1 1/2 cup large curd cottage cheese, drained

In a container with a screw top lid combine sugar, onion, oil, vinegar, poppy seeds, salt, and mustard. Shake well to mix. Divide recipe in half; mix cottage cheese with half of the dressing. Refrigerate until ready to serve. Just before serving, mix the cottage cheese mixture with the spinach salad. Pour remaining dressing over top to moisten.

JICAMA AND RED SWEET PEPPER SALAD

1 large jicama, peeled and cut into thin strips
1 sweet red pepper, cored, seeded, cut into thin strips
chopped cilantro, to taste
2 scallions, thinly sliced
1 clove garlic, minced

Dressing
2 tablespoons lemon juice
2 to 3 drops of Tabasco sauce
1/2 teaspoon salt
1/2 teaspoon sugar
4 tablespoons olive oil

In a large bowl combine jicama, red pepper, cilantro, scallions and garlic. For the dressing, in a small bowl combine lemon juice, hot sauce, salt and sugar; mix well and continue to mix while drizzling in the olive oil. Pour over vegetable mixture and toss until well coated.

Herb Long, Peculiar, Missouri, adapted this from a recipe he saw on a cooking show on KCPT. He makes it for his family every Christmas and serves as an accompaniment to Green Chile Stew (page 117).

BROCCOLI SLAW

2 packages beef-flavored ramen noodles
1 (1-pound) package broccoli slaw
2 bunches green onions, sliced
1 cup slivered almonds
1 cup sunflower seed meats

Dressing
1 cup salad oil
1/2 cup sugar
1/3 cup red wine vinegar

Cook ramen noodles according to package directions. Set flavor packets aside. Drain noodles and add to broccoli slaw. Add onions, almonds and sunflower seeds. Toss to mix. Set salad aside. For dressing, in a small bowl combine the two beef flavor packets with oil, sugar and vinegar. Pour over the slaw mixture and refrigerate overnight.

"I got this recipe years ago from a friend who made it with cabbage. Everyone who has eaten this loves it and demands the recipe. I've tried it as both cabbage and broccoli slaw—and prefer the broccoli."
Maxine N. Howard
Kansas City, Missouri

RED, WHITE AND GREEN BEAN SALAD

What's red, white and green and welcome at picnics all over town? Leigh Peterman, Kansas City, Missouri, knows— it's this tangy salad that's as good to look at as it is to eat.

1 pound whole fresh green beans,
**   steamed until just tender, 4 to 6 minutes**
1 (16-ounce) can garbanzo beans, drained
2 medium tomatoes, diced
1/2 cup thinly sliced red onion

Dressing
1/3 cup fresh lemon juice
1 tablespoon olive oil
1/2 teaspoon salt
1/4 teaspoon pepper
1/2 teaspoon sugar

In large bowl combine green beans, garbanzo beans, tomatoes and red onion. For dressing, in small bowl whisk together all dressing ingredients; pour over salad. Cover and chill 4 to 24 hours, stirring occasionally. Serve chilled.

MARINATED VEGETABLE SALAD

Barbara Wacker, Leavenworth, Kansas, keeps a variety of canned vegetables on hand ready for a salad that can be quickly assembled. She uses the marinade on kidney beans, asparagus, or whatever the pantry yields.

Marinade
3/4 cup vinegar
3/4 cup sugar
1 tablespoon water
1 teaspoon salt
1/4 to 1/2 teaspoon pepper

1 (17-ounce) can baby peas, drained
1 (12-ounce) can shoe peg corn, drained
1 (2-ounce) jar diced pimiento, drained
1 cup finely chopped celery
1 cup finely chopped onion

In a small saucepan combine marinade ingredients; bring mixture to a boil and boil one minute. Let cool completely. Combine salad ingredients in a bowl, and toss lightly. Pour marinade over vegetable mixture; stir gently. Cover salad and refrigerate overnight. Makes 6 servings.

HOMINY SALAD

1 (16-ounce) can white hominy, drained
1 (16-ounce) can yellow hominy, drained
1 cup chopped green pepper
1 cup chopped red pepper
1 cup chopped onion
1 cup chopped fresh tomato
1 cup chopped celery
1/2 cup vinegar
1 cup sugar
salt and pepper to taste

Combine all ingredients. Refrigerate for 2 to 24 hours before serving. Makes 6 servings.

Pauline Van Slyke, Kansas City, Missouri, likes to make this in the summertime as an alternative to potato salad. It really tastes best, she says, if allowed to sit overnight before serving.

MARINATED BLACK-EYED PEAS

1/2 cup vinegar
1/2 cup sugar
1/2 cup vegetable oil
1/2 medium red onion, sliced or diced
1 teaspoon chili powder
1 small jar chopped pimientos
1/2 teaspoon salt
1 teaspoon pepper
2 cloves garlic, crushed and left whole
3 (16-ounce) cans black-eyed peas, drained and washed

In a medium container with screw-top lid, combine all ingredients except black-eyed peas. Shake well to blend. Pour mixture over the peas. Cover and refrigerate at least over night. Remove garlic before serving. Makes 8 servings.

Many Kansas Citians consider black-eyed peas "good luck" fare and serve them on New Years Day. Carol Belt, Kansas City, Missouri, makes this recipe all year round and likes to garnish with a few thin lemon slices.

SPICY BLACK BEAN SALAD WITH LIME VINAIGRETTE

"Can't remember who gave me this recipe, but I've made the salad a lot and people who taste it always ask for a copy. Great for picnics and potlucks."
Teri Bavley
Prairie Village, Kansas

3 (15-ounce) cans black beans, drained and rinsed
1 red onion, minced
2 large ripe tomatoes, chopped
1/2 cup fresh cilantro, chopped
3 jalapeno peppers, seeded and minced

Lime Vinaigrette
2 tablespoons lime juice
1 1/2 teaspoons cumin
1 tablespoon red wine vinegar
1/2 cup olive oil
1 teaspoon salt
1/2 teaspoon freshly-ground pepper

In a large bowl combine beans, onion, tomatoes, cilantro and peppers. For the vinaigrette, in a screw-top jar combine all vinaigrette ingredients, cover and shake well. Pour vinaigrette over bean mixture and toss gently until well mixed. Refrigerate for 4 to 24 hours before serving. Makes 8 servings.

WESTON FOURTH OF JULY POTATO SALAD

"My daughter-in-law, Raleigh Hull Lang, grew up in Weston. Celebrating the 4th there has become a tradition. We love this potato salad!
Beverly Lang
Overland Park, KS

1 quart mayonnaise
2 pounds small curd cottage cheese
1 tablespoon prepared mustard
1 tablespoon parsley
1 teaspoon caraway seed
5 pounds potatoes, peeled, cooked, and diced
1 large red onion, chopped
1 cup sliced celery
salt and pepper to taste

In a medium bowl combine mayonnaise, cottage cheese, mustard, parsley and caraway seed. In the bottom of a dish, place a layer of half of the potatoes, onions and celery. Cover with half of the mayonnaise mixture, add salt and pepper. Repeat layers. Refrigerate 24 hours. Stir before serving. Makes 1 1/2 gallons.

RED POTATO AND BACON SALAD WITH GARLIC DRESSING

Garlic Dressing
2 cups mayonnaise (use only real mayonnaise)
4 to 6 cloves garlic, minced
1/4 cup minced fresh parsley
2 tablespoons Dijon-style mustard
1 teaspoon salt
1/2 teaspoon pepper

3 pounds red potatoes, cooked and diced
1 pound bacon, cooked and crumbled
1 (10-ounce) package frozen peas, thawed and drained
1 cup thinly-sliced green onion tops

In small bowl blend dressing ingredients. Cover and chill 4 to 24 hours. In medium bowl combine salad ingredients. Toss with dressing while potatoes are warm. Cover and chill several hours or overnight. Makes 8 servings.

KCPT *ip: Serve this light and tangy version of potato salad at your next patio party! Bake, cool and cut 6 medium potatoes into 1/4 inch slices (leaving skins on); place in large bowl. For the dressing, whisk together 1/2 cup olive oil, 1/2 cup cider vinegar, 4 tablespoons capers, 1/4 cup chopped fresh rosemary and 1 clove garlic, minced. Pour dressing over all, toss to cover; salt and pepper to taste.*

"It's the garlic that makes the difference," says June Lewallen of Basehor, Kansas, about this hearty potato salad that's one of her favorite recipes.

THE BEST WURST POTATO SALAD WITH WARM BACON DRESSING

Lucylle Perry of Kansas City, Kansas, makes the "wurst" potato salad and everyone loves it! She sometimes substitutes bratwurst for the smoked sausage.

2 pounds whole tiny new potatoes, cut in quarters
8 ounces fully cooked smoked sausage

Warm Bacon Dressing
6 strips bacon, chopped
1/4 cup chopped onion
1/4 cup chopped celery
1 tablespoon bacon drippings
1/4 cup water
3 tablespoons sugar
1/2 cup vinegar
1 (16-ounce) can sauerkraut, drained and rinsed
celery leaves, optional

Place a steamer basket in a large saucepan. Add water to just below bottom of basket. Bring water to a boil. Place potatoes and sausage in basket. Steam for 20 to 25 minutes, until potatoes are tender. Drain. Cool sausage slightly. Slice diagonally into 1-inch pieces. For the dressing, cook bacon, onion and celery until brown. Drain. Reserve 1 tablespoon drippings. Add water to drippings and add back to bacon, onion and celery along with the sugar and vinegar. Simmer five minutes until slightly thickened. Stir in sauerkraut. Combine potatoes, sausage and dressing; toss to coat. Top with celery leaves. Serve warm. Makes 12 to 14 side-dish servings.

HOT BAKED POTATO SALAD

8 medium baking potatoes, peeled, cooked and diced
1 pound cheddar cheese, cubed or shredded
1 cup mayonnaise or salad dressing
1/2 cup chopped onions
salt and pepper to taste
1/2 pound partially fried chopped bacon, drained
1/2 cup sliced black olives

In a large bowl combine potatoes, cheese, mayonnaise, onion, salt and pepper; place in a buttered casserole. Top with bacon and olives. Bake one hour at 325 degrees. Makes 6 servings.

Potato salad—it's not just for summer anymore! Not when you use this luscious recipe from Sandra Famuliner of Carrollton, Missouri. Try it as a buffet item, then sit back and accept the compliments.

GREEK STYLE COUSCOUS SALAD

2/3 cup couscous
1 cup boiling water
3/4 cup canned garbanzo beans, drained (chick-peas)
1/2 cup chopped yellow or red bell pepper
1/3 cup sliced, pitted black olives
1/3 cup chopped red onion
3 tablespoons chopped fresh mint
3 tablespoons olive oil
2 tablespoons fresh lemon juice
3/4 cup crumbled feta cheese (about 3 ounces)

Place couscous in medium bowl. Pour boiling water over and stir to combine. Set aside until couscous is soft and water is absorbed, about 10 minutes. Fluff couscous with fork. Add garbanzo beans, bell pepper, olives, onion and mint; toss lightly. Mix in olive oil and lemon juice, then feta cheese. Season to taste with salt and pepper. Refrigerate until ready to serve. Makes 2 servings.

Jane Wagner, Kansas City, Missouri, first made this dish because it went together so fast. She continues to do so because it simply tastes so good. Jane likes to serve it at home with grilled fish. When she takes it out for a potluck, she doubles or triples the recipe.

KCPT *ip: Create your own garden couscous by replacing the garbanzo beans with fresh chopped tomatoes, green onions and sliced squash.*

ROTINI NICOISE
WITH LEMON VINAIGRETTE

Mary Pfeifer Langley, Kansas City, Missouri, adapted this recipe from one she obtained in an "on-line" cooking conversation! It has become a favorite summertime dish.

Lemon Vinaigrette
1/4 cup olive oil
1/2 cup low-sodium chicken broth
1/2 cup freshly squeezed lemon juice
2 cloves garlic, minced
2 teaspoons Dijon-style mustard
1 teaspoon salt
1/2 teaspoon freshly-ground black pepper

1 pound rotini pasta, uncooked
2 cups canned white beans (cannellini), rinsed and
    drained
2 cups cooked chicken breast meat, cut into chunks
1 (14-ounce) can artichoke hearts packed in water,
    drained
12 cherry tomatoes, for garnish
8 ounces green beans, blanched and refreshed,
    for garnish
16 black olives, for garnish

For the vinaigrette, in a medium bowl whisk together all ingredients. Set aside.

Prepare pasta according to package directions; drain, rinse again under cold water, drain thoroughly and put in a large mixing bowl. Add white beans, chicken and artichoke hearts and toss well. Pour vinaigrette over pasta mixture and toss well. To serve, spoon pasta on large serving platter or bowl and arrange tomatoes, green beans and olives around and on top. Makes 6 servings.

KCPT *ip: Substitute 2 cups fresh blanched broccoli for the artichoke.*

PATIO MACARONI SALAD

4 ounces macaroni, cooked and drained
2 boiled eggs, chopped
6 slices bacon, crisped and crumbled
1/2 cup chopped celery
3 tablespoons chopped green pepper
2 tablespoons chopped green onion
1/4 cup sliced black olives
1 teaspoon dry parsley
1/2 cup shredded cheddar cheese
2 tablespoons pickle relish
1/2 cup mayonnaise
1 1/2 teaspoons sugar
cream to thin
salt and pepper to taste

In a large bowl combine macaroni, eggs, bacon, celery, green pepper, onion, olives, parsley, cheese, and pickle relish, stirring to mix well. Combine mayonnaise, sugar and enough cream to thin a bit; add to macaroni mixture, stirring to coat everything well. Add salt and pepper. Refrigerate until ready to serve. Makes 4 servings.

Whether it's a family dinner on the patio or a potluck picnic, this salad is always welcome. Rita Downey, Raymore, Missouri, says this is one of her summer "standby" recipes.

FIVE-CUP SALAD

1 cup pineapple chunks
1 cup mandarin orange segments
1 cup miniature marshmallows
1 cup coconut
1 cup sour cream

In a medium bowl combine all ingredients, mixing lightly. Cover and refrigerate for 2 to 24 hours before serving.

KCPT *ip: For a deluxe version of this popular salad, Wanda Riordan of Pleasant Hill whips one cup of cream and adds after combining all other ingredients—making it "Six Cup Salad."*

When Debbie Globoke, Belton, Missouri, serves this old family favorite recipe, she likes to prepare well in advance and let sit at least overnight.

SAUCY CHERRY LAYERED SALAD

2 small packages cherry-flavored gelatin, divided
2 cups boiling water, divided
2 cups applesauce, divided
1 cup sour cream
1 (8-ounce) package cream cheese
1 cup chopped pecans
3/4 cup chopped celery

For first layer, dissolve 1 package of gelatin in 1 cup of boiling water; cool. Stir in one cup applesauce. Pour into 8 x 10 pan; refrigerate until set, approximately 1 to 2 hours. For second layer, combine sour cream, cream cheese, pecans and celery. Spread on top of first layer; refrigerate approximately 1 to 2 hours. For third layer, repeat instructions for first layer. Spread on top of second layer; refrigerate until set, 1 to 2 hours. Makes 8 servings.

FROZEN CRANBERRY SALAD

16 ounces cranberries
2 cups sugar
16 ounces miniature marshmallows
1 (20-ounce) can crushed pineapple, drained
1 pint whipping cream, whipped

Chop cranberries in blender or food processor. In small bowl mix with sugar; cover and refrigerate overnight. In another bowl combine marshmallows and pineapple; cover and refrigerate overnight. Combine the above ingredients; fold in whipped cream. Place into two 9-inch square pans. Freeze for 24 hours.

KEPT*ip: Betty Payne, Gladstone, Missouri, makes a "hurry-up" version of this salad by combining 1 (20-ounce) can whole cranberry sauce, 1 (20-ounce) can drained pineapple, 1 (20-ounce) can cherry pie filling, 1 (14-ounce) can sweetened evaporated milk and 1 (12-ounce) carton of whipped topping.*

Vegetables & Side Dishes

The many good farmers' markets of Kansas City keep us well supplied with locally-grown produce in the summertime. And when that growing season has ceased, first-class grocery stores provide whatever we need. With the wealth of good ingredients to choose from, Kansas Citians excel at memorable side dishes and vegetables—one of the hallmarks of great home cooking!

Asparagus with Lemon and Hazelnut Oil

Carrots Provencal

Corn Bake

Eggplant with Tomato Sauce

Green Beans Sicilian Style

Yellow Squash Casserole

Scalloped Tomatoes with Garlic and Basil

Spoon Bread

Cheese and Garlic Grits

Potatoes Blue

Potatoes with Two Cheeses

Potatoes Royale

Sweet Potato Casserole

Confetti Rice

Persian Green Rice with Lima Beans

Black Beans and Rice

Baked Pineapple

Grandma's Apple Butter

...and more!

ASPARAGUS WITH LEMON HAZELNUT OIL

1 tablespoon butter
32 fresh asparagus spears, blanched or steamed for
  2 minutes
3 ounces hazelnut oil
2 tablespoons lemon juice, or juice of 1/2 lemon
Salt and pepper to taste

Lightly sauté asparagus in butter over medium heat for 3 to 4 minutes. Add hazelnut oil, lemon juice, salt and pepper. Serve immediately. Makes 4 servings.

To take advantage of the flavor only fresh asparagus can provide, Sarah Crooks, Shawnee Mission, Kansas, believes in keeping the preparation simple. Try varying the flavor of the oil.

CARROTS PROVENCAL

2 tablespoons extra virgin olive oil
2 pounds baby carrots
4 to 6 garlic cloves, peeled and halved
Salt to taste
30 best-quality black olives, pitted and halved

In large skillet heat oil over medium-high heat until hot. Add the carrots, stirring to coat with oil. Reduce heat to medium; cover and braise for 20 minutes, stirring frequently. Add the garlic, season with salt and stir. Reduce heat to low and continue cooking until the carrots are almost caramelized and the garlic is soft and tender, about 15 minutes more. Sprinkle with the olives, stir, and taste for seasoning. Serve hot or at room temperature. Makes 8 to 10 servings.

Barbro Lucas, of Fairway, Kansas, prefers to use Kalamata olives for this unique dish. Because it can be served at room temperature, it makes a perfect addition to a buffet.

EGGPLANT WITH TOMATO SAUCE

1 large eggplant, peeled and cut into 1/2-inch slices
6 tablespoons olive oil, divided
2 cloves of garlic, chopped
2 basil leaves
1 (28-ounce) can diced tomatoes
Salt and pepper to taste
1 cup freshly grated romano cheese

Sprinkle salt on both sides of each slice of eggplant and let stand on paper towels for 30 minutes. Squeeze until liquid is drained out. In a large pan fry slices of eggplant in 3 tablespoons of the olive oil until well browned; remove from pan. In the same pan heat the remaining 3 tablespoons of olive oil. Combine the garlic, basil leaves, tomatoes, salt and pepper and cook in the hot oil for 5 to 10 minutes. Place half the eggplant slices on a large platter, cover with half the tomato sauce then 1/2 cup of the cheese. Repeat layers. Serve immediately. Makes 6 servings.

GREEN BEANS SICILIAN STYLE

2 cloves garlic, chopped
3 tablespoons olive oil
1 pound green beans, trimmed and blanched for
   2 to 3 minutes
1/4 cup bread crumbs
1/4 cup freshly grated romano cheese

In a large pan sauté garlic in oil until golden brown. Add beans. Combine bread crumbs and cheese and add to the pan. Cook 5 minutes on low heat. Serve hot. Makes 6 servings.

"My mother, Lucille Valenti-Mandacina, cooked with the recipes my grandmother brought from Italy. I was an adult before I realized we'd grown up eating healthily—long before it was trendy. Mother worked in a factory in the north end of Kansas City near our home. She had to cook dishes that could be prepared quickly, and we always had an array of fresh vegetables. Mother used very little salt, but her recipes almost always included cheese, and it was always romano cheese!"
Roselyn Kraack
Kansas City, Missouri

CORN BAKE

1/2 cup (1 stick) butter
1/4 cup chopped onion
1/2 cup chopped green bell pepper
1 (16-ounce) can whole kernel corn, with liquid
1 (16-ounce) can cream style corn
1 (8 1/2-ounce) package corn muffin mix
3 eggs, slightly beaten
3/4 cup sour cream
1 cup shredded cheddar cheese

In a small saucepan cook onion and green pepper in butter until tender. Combine all ingredients and pour into a lightly greased 3-quart baking dish. Bake 45 minutes at 350 degrees. Makes 8 servings.

YELLOW SQUASH CASSEROLE

2 pounds yellow squash, sliced and seeded (do not peel)
1 cup water
2 small onions, chopped
2 tablespoons margarine, melted
1 1/2 cups shredded cheddar cheese
2 eggs, beaten
1 strip bacon, cooked and crumbled
2 ounces chopped pimento, drained (optional)
1/4 teaspoon salt
1/4 teaspoon pepper
1 cup plus 2 tablespoons buttery cracker crumbs

In large pan simmer squash in water until just tender. Drain well. Add remaining ingredients, reserving 2 tablespoons of crumbs. Stir to combine and spoon into buttered casserole. Sprinkle reserved crumbs on top. Bake at 350 degrees for 20 to 30 minutes, until cheese is melted and bubbly. Makes 6 servings.

Susan Hornung of Mission Hills, Kansas is known among her friends as a terrific cook. Corn Bake is a dish that she likes to prepare for buffet dinners.

"We grow squash and this is a dish I make a lot. Everyone in my family likes it—and it's just as good the next day; I think better. The reason I simmer or parboil the squash first is to cut down baking time on hot summer days. You could also make this with zucchini."
Pauline Van Slyke
Kansas City,
Missouri

SCALLOPED TOMATOES
WITH GARLIC AND BASIL

"This delicious casserole can be a side dish or serve as the main dish for a meatless meal. My husband, Richard, and I often have it for dinner. Add a bottle of good wine and a green salad for a memorable food experience."
Roxanne Wyss
Olathe, Kansas

4 tablespoons olive oil, divided
2 cups French bread, cut into 1/2-inch cubes
16 ripe plum tomatoes, cut into 1/2-inch cubes
3 cloves garlic, minced
1 tablespoon sugar
Salt and pepper to taste
1/4 cup shredded basil leaves
3 tablespoons parmesan cheese

Heat oil in large nonstick skillet. Add bread cubes and stir to coat; cook over medium heat 5 to 7 minutes or until bread is lightly browned. Stir in tomatoes and garlic. Sprinkle with sugar. Cook 5 minutes, stirring frequently. Season with salt and pepper, then stir in basil and remove from heat. Transfer tomato mixture to 1 1/2-quart casserole. Sprinkle with cheese and drizzle with remaining oil. Bake at 350 degrees for 35 to 40 minutes or until bubbling and lightly browned. Makes 6 servings.

SPOON BREAD

2 1/4 cups milk
2 tablespoons butter
1 teaspoon salt
2/3 cup yellow cornmeal
3 eggs, separated

In medium pan heat milk, butter and salt until scalding, stirring occasionally. Slowly stir in cornmeal. Cook for 1 minute, stirring constantly. Remove from heat and cool for a few minutes. Beat egg yolks; stir cornmeal mixture into egg yolks. Beat egg whites until stiff; fold into cornmeal mixture. Pour into lightly greased 1 1/2-quart casserole dish. Bake at 375 degrees for 35 to 45 minutes. Remove from oven just before center is firm; the dish will continue to cook after removed from oven. Serve with spoon from baking dish; pass with plenty of butter. Makes 6 servings.

CHEESE AND GARLIC GRITS

1/2 cup (1 stick) butter
1 (8-ounce) garlic cheese roll
2 eggs
Milk
1 cup quick-cooking grits, prepared according to package directions
2 cloves fresh garlic, crushed
1/2 cup buttered bread crumbs (optional)
1/2 cup shredded cheddar cheese (optional)

In small pan melt butter and cheese roll over low heat. Beat eggs well and place in measuring cup; add enough milk to fill to 1 cup. Combine grits, cheese, egg mixture and garlic. Pour mixture into lightly greased 1 1/2-quart baking dish. Sprinkle with bread crumbs and/or shredded cheese. Bake at 350 degrees for 40 minutes, or until firm. Makes 4 to 6 servings.

"Many of our family recipes are my great grandmother's who lived near Fredericksburg, Virginia. When Mother made this, all the kids in the neighborhood came to dinner."
Joyce Ann Jaillite Independence, Missouri

"My Derby Day party wouldn't be complete without these grits. I've had many requests for the recipe. I am always asked to make it for holiday dinners when I visit my family in Wisconsin!"
Mary Loberg Overland Park, Kansas

POTATOES ROYALE

4 medium potatoes, thinly sliced
1/4 cup chopped onion
1/4 cup water
1/2 cup butter, melted
1/3 cup sour cream
1 cup shredded cheddar cheese
1/4 cup sliced black olives
1/2 teaspoon salt
Dash pepper
4 slices bacon, cooked and crumbled

Place potatoes in a 1 1/2-quart baking dish; add onions and water. Cover and microwave until tender, about 14 to 15 minutes, stirring twice. In small bowl combine butter, sour cream, cheese, olives, salt and pepper. Add to potatoes and stir gently to combine. Sprinkle bacon on top. Microwave until heated through. Makes 4 to 6 servings.

BAKED MASHED POTATOES

1 (8-ounce) package cream cheese
1 cup half and half
5 pounds red potatoes, peeled and cooked
3/4 cup (1 1/2 sticks) butter, divided
1 teaspoon onion salt
1 teaspoon salt
1/4 teaspoon pepper
Paprika

In mixing bowl combine cream cheese and half and half; mix well. Add hot potatoes, 1/2 cup butter, onion salt, salt and pepper; mix until light and fluffy. Transfer to 2-quart casserole. Melt the remaining 1/4 cup butter and brush on top of potatoes. Sprinkle with paprika. Bake at 350 degrees for 30 minutes. Makes 10 to 12 servings.

POTATOES WITH TWO CHEESES

1 pound (3 medium) red potatoes, peeled and cut into
    thin slices
1/4 cup extra virgin olive oil, divided
1/2 teaspoon salt
2 cloves garlic, chopped
1/4 cup flat leaf Italian parsley, chopped
Freshly ground black pepper to taste
3/4 cup grated parmesan cheese
1/3 cup fine dry bread crumbs, divided
8 ounces shredded mozzarella cheese

Joseph J. Roh enjoys entertaining in his Leawood, Kansas, home. This delicious potato dish is one he often prepares to accompany his grilled lamb (page 69).

In medium bowl toss potatoes with 2 tablespoons olive oil. Sprinkle with salt and toss to season. In small bowl mix garlic, parsley, pepper and parmesan cheese. Sprinkle 3 tablespoons of the bread crumbs in the bottom of a lightly oiled 1 1/2-quart baking dish. Place one-third of the potatoes in the bottom of the dish, overlapping slightly to fit. Spread half of the cheese mixture over potatoes, then half of the mozzarella cheese. Add another one-third of the potatoes, then the remaining parmesan and the remaining mozzarella. Top this with the remaining potatoes. Sprinkle the remaining bread crumbs on top and drizzle with the remaining olive oil. Bake at 400 degrees for 50 to 60 minutes or until potatoes are tender. Remove from oven and allow to sit a few minutes before serving. Makes 6 servings.

KCPT *ip: Mark Ronfeldt, of Shawnee Mission, Kansas, prefers "Potatoes Blue." To try Mark's version of "Baked Mashed Potatoes" (page 44), eliminate cream cheese and substitute 5 ounces of blue cheese and 5 or 6 cloves of finely minced garlic. Reduce onion salt to 1/2 teaspoon or eliminate, according to taste.*

STEPHANIE'S BEST TWICE-BAKED POTATOES

6 large baking potatoes
1 cup (2 sticks) butter, divided
1 cup heavy whipping cream
Salt and cracked pepper to taste
1/2 cup shredded gruyere cheese

Wash and dry potatoes; do not oil or wrap in foil. Bake at 400 degrees for 1 hour or until done. Cut slice from top of each potato and scoop out pulp. In a large bowl combine potato pulp and 3/4 cup butter. Stir lightly until butter begins to melt; do not mash. Add whipping cream, salt and pepper. Stir lightly. Place potatoes in a 3-quart baking dish. Dot top with remaining butter; sprinkle cheese on top. Bake uncovered at 350 degrees for 25 to 30 minutes. Makes 6 to 8 servings.

SWEET POTATO CASSEROLE

3 cups cooked and mashed sweet potatoes
1 cup (2 sticks) butter, at room temperature, divided
1 cup sugar, divided
Nutmeg to taste
Cinnamon to taste
1 cup chopped pecans
1/3 cup flour

In large bowl combine sweet potatoes, 1/2 cup butter, 1/2 cup sugar, nutmeg and cinnamon. Place in lightly greased 2-quart casserole. In medium bowl combine pecans, flour and remaining butter and sugar: stir to mix. Spread on top of sweet potatoes. Bake at 350 degrees for 35 minutes. Makes 8 to 10 servings.

TURKEY DRESSING

Turkey Broth
Neck, gizzard and liver from turkey
1 carrot, sliced
1 stalk celery, sliced
2 1/2 cups water

1 loaf white bread, toasted and broken into bite size
**   pieces**
Recipe for 9-inch pan corn bread, prepared and
**   crumbled into pieces**
1 1/2 cups raisins
1 1/2 cups (3 sticks) butter or margarine
1 onion, finely chopped
2 cups diced celery
2/3 cup milk
2 eggs, beaten
2 teaspoons salt
1 teaspoon pepper
2 tablespoons poultry seasoning

Place the turkey parts, carrot, celery and water in a large pan. Simmer about 1 hour. Strain broth, reserve 2 cups for dressing. In a very large bowl combine white bread pieces, corn bread pieces, and raisins. In a medium pan cook onions and celery in butter or margarine until tender. Add milk, reserved broth and eggs. Gradually add liquid mixture to bread and raisins, stirring to mix. Bread should be moist but not mushy. Season to taste with salt, pepper and poultry seasoning. Place several cups of the dressing in turkey for baking. Place remaining dressing in lightly greased baking dish. Bake at 325 degrees for 45 minutes. Makes 10 servings.

"This is the first recipe my mother-in-law, Clara Wallace, shared with me. Now it's a standard part of our holiday dinners."
Sally Wallace
Fairway, Kansas

CONFETTI RICE

"You can use regular white rice, but if you've never eaten Basmati rice, you're in for a treat. Once you taste it, you'll be hooked!"
Bonnie Jones
Independence,
Missouri

4 tablespoons butter
1 cup diced green bell pepper
1 cup diced red bell pepper
1 cup diced yellow onion
4 cloves minced garlic
2 cups uncooked Basmati rice
1/2 teaspoon ground oregano
1 teaspoon ground cumin
4 cups hot water
4 teaspoons chicken stock granules
1 teaspoon salt
2 tablespoons chopped fresh parsley or cilantro

In a large heavy skillet melt the butter over medium-high heat. Add the diced peppers, onion, garlic, rice, oregano and cumin. Sauté and stir constantly until the rice looks well-glazed and is slightly golden. Add the hot water, chicken stock granules, salt and parsley or cilantro; bring to a slight boil. Reduce heat to medium-low and simmer, tightly covered, 20 minutes; do not peek or stir! Remove from heat. Remove the lid, stir very gently, and set lid ajar to allow the rice to fluff for 5 minutes. Makes 12 servings.

PERSIAN GREEN RICE
WITH LIMA BEANS

1 quart plus 3 1/4 cups water, divided
2 1/2 teaspoons salt, divided
2 cups basmati rice, washed
8 ounces frozen baby lima beans
2 tablespoons dried dill weed
1/4 to 1/2 teaspoon powdered saffron, optional
3 tablespoons olive oil, divided
2 medium potatoes, peeled and sliced

In large pan heat one quart water to warm. Add 2 teaspoons salt and rice; soak for 1 to 2 hours. Drain. In same pan bring 3 cups of water to boil. Add rice and remaining 1/2 teaspoon salt. Cover and continue to boil over medium-high heat until half-cooked, about 15 minutes. Drain rice and rinse with cold water. In small pan sauté lima beans, dill weed and optional saffron in 1 tablespoon olive oil 5 to 7 minutes. In larger pan sauté potatoes in 2 tablespoons olive oil for 15 minutes. Combine lima beans and rice; layer on top of potatoes. Pour 1/4 cup water over top. Cover pan and steam over low heat for 1 hour until rice is done. Makes 6 servings.

"Green rice is very popular in my native Persia and is often served with fish or chicken. This is always a favorite dish when served at large gatherings."
Shirin Khodayari
Overland Park, Kansas

BLACK BEANS AND RICE

Chef Peter Castillo grew up in Miami with a mother who cooked fabulous Caribbean dishes. Some of those were on the menu of Peter's restaurant in Lenexa, Kansas. Now he shares with KCPT members.

1/2 cup olive oil, divided
1 large onion, diced
1 green bell pepper, diced
Dash oregano
2 cups rice
1 cup black beans, cooked until tender
1 bay leaf
2 tablespoons green olive brine
4 cups water

In large pan sauté onion and pepper in 2 tablespoons olive oil until tender. Add oregano and rice and cook for 5 minutes. Add beans, remaining olive oil, bay leaf and olive brine. Add water; cover with a paper towel between pan and lid. Cook for 30 minutes, stirring occasionally in an outward motion, until rice is tender. Keep covered until ready to serve. Makes 10 servings.

KCPT *ip: When preparing rice, make a double batch. Freeze in 1-cup portions for salad or to thicken a soup. Leftover rice is also the basis of great fried rice. Bring rice to room temperature; sauté in a little olive oil with chopped meat, mushrooms, green onions, ginger root, dash of soy sauce—whatever sounds good!*

WESTON BAKED BEANS

1 (15-ounce) can kidney beans, drained
1 (15-ounce) can pinto beans or baby lima beans,
   drained
1 (16-ounce) can pork and beans
6 sliced bacon, chopped and slightly cooked
1/2 cup catsup
1/2 cup brown sugar
1/2 teaspoon chili powder
1/4 teaspoon cumin
1/8 teaspoon cinnamon
1 medium onion, chopped
1 cup shredded cheddar cheese

In large bowl combine all ingredients except cheese. Pour into lightly buttered bean pot or 3-quart casserole. Bake uncovered at 400 degrees for 45 minutes. Sprinkle cheese on top, cover and bake for 15 minutes more. Makes 12 servings.

"I first tasted these beans at a Fourth of July celebration Now we enjoy them all year round at family gatherings. The beans go especially well with barbecue."
Beverly Lang
Overland Park, Kansas

BAKED PINEAPPLE

1 egg, beaten
1/2 cup sugar
2 tablespoons flour
1/2 cup bread crumbs
4 ounces cheddar cheese, diced
1 (20-ounce) can pineapple chunks, drained, reserve juice

In small pan combine egg, sugar, flour, bread crumbs and reserved pineapple juice. Cook over medium heat, stirring constantly, until thick. Remove from heat and stir in cheese until partially melted. Stir in pineapple. Place in buttered 1 1/2-quart casserole. Bake at 350 degrees for 30 minutes until brown. Makes 4 to 6 servings.

MUSHROOM PIE

1/2 cup (1 stick) butter
1 pound fresh mushrooms, sliced
3 tablespoons flour
1 can mushroom soup
1 cup milk
Salt to taste
Pastry for double crust pie

In a heavy skillet sauté the mushrooms lightly in butter. Sprinkle flour on top of the mushrooms and stir so that the flour cooks into the butter. Combine the soup and milk, then add slowly to the mushrooms; stir to mix well. Add salt to taste. Cook over medium heat until the mixture is fairly thick. Place bottom pie crust in a 9-inch pie pan. Pour mushroom mixture into pie shell. Fit top crust over filling, seal and flute edges. Make slits in top crust to vent. Bake at 350 degrees for 45 minutes, or until crust is golden brown. Makes 8 servings.

AROMATIC MUSHROOMS

4 pounds fresh mushrooms
1 pound (4 sticks) butter
1 quart burgundy
1 1/2 tablespoons worcestershire sauce
1 teaspoon dill weed
1 teaspoon pepper
2 cups boiling water
4 teaspoons beef flavor base
4 teaspoons chicken flavor base

In large pan combine all ingredients. Bring to a boil. Reduce heat, cover and simmer 5 to 6 hours. Remove cover and continue to simmer 3 to 5 hours more, until liquid is reduced to about half. Makes 12 servings.

Lois Hunt, of Prairie Village, Kansas, serves these mushrooms with beef tenderloin. She got this recipe from her friend, Peg Anderson-Lee, who uses it as an appetizer.

CRANBERRY WALNUT RELISH

1 (16-ounce) bag fresh cranberries
2 1/2 cups sugar
1/2 teaspoon cinnamon
1 cup orange marmalade
3 tablespoons lemon juice
1 cup coarsely broken English walnuts

Wash and drain berries. Place in 9 x 13 baking dish. Add sugar, cinnamon, marmalade and lemon juice; stir to combine. Cover tightly with foil and bake at 350 degrees for 1 hour. During last ten minutes of baking, toast walnuts on a baking sheet in oven. Add nuts to cranberry mixture; stir well. Cover and refrigerate for 2 to 24 hours. Makes 8 servings.

No feast is complete without cranberries! Sharon Mellor of Liberty, Missouri, says this relish is always a hit at her holiday dinners. She also serves it throughout the year with pork or poultry.

GRANDMA'S APPLE BUTTER

John Mertz and his daughter Laura of Shawnee, Kansas, make this apple butter every fall. The recipe came from John's Grandma Mertz who added the anise to give a traditional apple butter a bit of a kick!

1 1/2 gallons apple cider
8 pounds Jonathan apples, pared and quartered
3 cups sugar
1 1/2 teaspoons ground cinnamon
3/8 tablespoon anise

In very large pot boil cider, uncovered, until reduced to 3 quarts, about 1 hour and 15 minutes. Add apples; return to boil. Reduce heat and simmer, uncovered, until apples are soft, about 1 hour. Run mixture through food mill; return to pot. Add sugar, cinnamon and anise. Bring to a boil; reduce heat and simmer, uncovered, stirring frequently until no liquid separates from pulp, at least 2 hours. Cool to room temperature. Refrigerate, covered, for up to 2 weeks. Makes 6 to 7 cups.

LOU JANE'S "ROYAL JELLY" SAUCE

Lou Jane Temple of Kansas City, Missouri, is noted for her culinary mysteries. But it's no mystery why this unique barbecue sauce is a favorite with all her friends. The sauce also makes a tasty appetizer— just use to top cream cheese.

4 pickled peaches, pitted
6 to 10 cloves of roasted garlic
1 cup orange juice
1/2 cup apple cider vinegar
1/2 cup juice from jar of pickled peaches
1/2 cup honey mustard
1/2 cup yellow mustard
1/2 cup honey
1/2 cup tomato catsup
2 tablespoons hot pepper sauce
1 tablespoons dry mustard
1 tablespoon kosher salt
1 tablespoon ground white pepper

In bowl of food processor purée peaches and roasted garlic. In a heavy saucepan combine all remaining ingredients. Add puréed peaches. Simmer 20 to 30 minutes until sauce has thickened and turned a golden orange. Cool and refrigerate.

Meat & Main Dishes

The main event! Kansas Citians may savor sweets, delight in seasonal fruits and vegetables and be enthralled by the aroma of freshly-baked bread, but whether casual or formal, the main course of any meal still commands our attention. Tastes are diverse—whether we're slow-smoking ribs, grilling fish in a flash or simmering beef in a savory casserole, we enjoy preparing and sharing dishes that reflect our interest in good cookery!

Cort's Two-Step Barbecued Brisket

Sauerbraten

Beef Burgundy

Keshy Yena

Blue Ribbon Meat Loaf

Pork Tenderloin—Southern Comfort Style

Pork Piccata

Rich's Grilled Marinated Chicken

Cuban Style Fried Chicken

Garlic Chicken Romano

Venison Medallions with Garlic and Capers

Two-Hour Turkey

Barbecue Shrimp

Baked Catfish

Enchilaadas

Pasta with Smoked Turkey and Cilantro Pesto

Penne with Roasted Tomato Sauce

...and more!

CORT'S "TWO-STEP" BARBECUED BRISKET

1 whole brisket, trimmed (about 9 to 11 pounds)
1 recipe Dry Rub
1 (18-ounce) bottle barbecue sauce

Dry Rub
4 tablespoons paprika
2 tablespoons chili powder
2 tablespoons dark brown sugar
1 tablespoon ground black pepper
1 tablespoon ground oregano
1 tablespoon sugar
2 teaspoons cayenne pepper (optional)
1 teaspoon ground white pepper

Combine all rub ingredients in a small bowl. Apply rub generously to brisket, pressing down to make sure spices adhere. Meat should be completely covered. Wrap tightly in plastic wrap and refrigerate overnight. One hour prior to cooking, remove brisket, unwrap and let sit at room temperature. Grill-smoke brisket using your favorite method, fat side up, without removing lid for about 2 hours. Heat (indoor) oven to 300 degrees. Position brisket lengthwise in center of two 48-inch long pieces of extra-heavy-duty foil, which have been folded 2 or 3 times to form a 48 x 36 rectangle. Bring short edges over and fold, crimping tightly to seal. Repeat with long edges to seal completely. Place brisket on baking sheet; bake 3 to 3 1/2 hours until very tender. Remove from oven, loosen foil at one end to release steam and let sit for 30 minutes. Drain juices into large bowl; remove fat. Mix equal parts juices and barbecue sauce. Slice brisket on the bias across the grain, moisten slices with some of sauce mixture. Pass remaining sauce separately. Makes 12 to 16 servings.

KGPT*ip: For controlled smoke release, wrap 4 to 6 wood chunks (about 3 inches each) or 3 cups wood chips in double sheet of heavy-duty foil. Prick at least 6 holes in top of foil pouch to allow smoke to escape; place on top of ash-covered coals.*

"This traditional dry rub is also excellent for use on pork ribs or even chicken. If there's anyone in your crowd who can't abide hot food, reduce or eliminate the cayenne pepper altogether. About the cooking process, what it may lack in barbecue authenticity, it more than makes up for in results. Your guests will tell you it's the best brisket they've ever tasted!"
Cort Sinnes
Kansas City, Missouri

BRISKET IN BEER

"Apple juice or hard apple cider may be used in place of the beer; Granny Smith hard cider is particularly good. My mother developed this recipe, and it's one of my favorites."
Sarah Berkowitz
Kansas City,
Missouri

3-pound beef brisket
12 ounces beer
1/2 teaspoon freshly ground black pepper
1 onion, sliced and separated into rings
1/2 cup bottled chili sauce or barbecue sauce
2 cloves garlic, minced
3 tablespoons brown sugar
2 tablespoons flour
1/2 cup cold water

Marinate brisket in beer for several hours or overnight. Preheat oven to 350 degrees. Remove brisket from beer, reserve beer. Place brisket in baking dish and sprinkle with pepper. Arrange onion rings on top of brisket. Combine beer used for marinade with chili sauce, garlic and brown sugar; pour over brisket. Cover dish with lid or double thickness of foil and bake for 3 hours. Uncover and bake an additional 20 minutes or until brisket is tender. Remove from oven and place brisket on platter. Pour 1 1/2 cups of the cooking liquid into a small saucepan. Place flour and water in a small jar with a tight-fitting lid; cover and shake vigorously until well-blended and smooth. Add flour mixture gradually to cooking liquid, stirring constantly over medium-high heat. Bring to a boil, reduce heat and simmer for two minutes. Cover and set aside. Slice brisket diagonally across the grain and serve with gravy over prepared wide egg noodles or roasted potatoes. Makes 6 servings.

SAUERBRATEN

8 bay leaves
1 tablespoon allspice
1 teaspoon mustard seed
8 whole cloves
1 teaspoon white pepper
2 tablespoons salt
1 cup brown sugar
1 quart white vinegar
1 pint good sherry wine
2 large onions, chopped
5-pound boneless beef round rump roast
2 to 3 tablespoons cooking oil

Gravy
1 cup good sherry wine
1 cup flour
1 quart water
1 (4-ounce) can mushrooms, drained
Salt and pepper to taste

In a large bowl (or heavy plastic bag with zip-lock top) combine bay leaves, allspice, mustard seed, cloves, pepper, salt, sugar, vinegar, sherry, and onions. Add roast; cover and refrigerate. Marinate for three days, turning meat once each day. Remove meat from marinade; drain and discard marinade. In a large skillet brown meat on all sides in hot oil. Place in a roasting pan and bake, covered, at 375 degrees for four hours, basting once per hour. Remove roast from pan, set aside. Pour pan juices into a medium pan. Add sherry. Blend flour with water until smooth. Add to pan juices, stirring constantly over medium-high heat. Bring to a boil, reduce heat and continue to cook until thickened. Add mushrooms and salt and pepper to taste. Thinly slice meat and serve with gravy. Makes 12 servings.

KCPTip: *If meat is chilled, it slices better—so make ahead if possible.*

SMOKY CROCKED BEEF

3-pound boneless rump roast
1/3 to 1/2 (4-ounce) bottle liquid smoke
2 tablespoons sugar
1 tablespoon chili powder
Salt and pepper to taste
1 cup barbecue sauce

Using a paring knife, make several cuts into the roast and place in a crock pot. Pour liquid smoke gently over all the exposed surfaces of the roast. Sprinkle with sugar, chili powder, salt and pepper. Pour barbecue sauce on top. Cover and cook on low for 10 hours. Don't lift the lid! Remove roast from crock pot and slice thinly. Serve with juice from crock pot or more barbecue sauce. Makes 6 to 8 servings.

"The aroma sends busy teenagers (and even hungry pets) running to the kitchen! This makes great sandwiches the second day."
Millie Krna
Kansas City, Missouri

GOOD & EASY ROAST BEEF

1 sirloin tip roast
Salt (or garlic salt) and pepper to taste

Preheat oven to 500 degrees. Sprinkle salt and pepper on roast. Place roast on rack in roasting pan. Bake for 4 to 5 minutes per pound. Turn oven off. Do not open door for 1 1/2 hours. Makes 6 to 8 servings.

Try this—it will be the easiest and best roast you've ever eaten. Truly makes a simple roast taste like steak."
Barbara Scanlon
Kansas City, Missouri

KESHY YENA

2 pounds round steak, cut into thin strips
1/4 cup plus 2 tablespoons flour
1/2 teaspoon salt
1/2 teaspoon black pepper, divided
3/4 cup butter, divided
1/2 cup red wine
2 green bell peppers, finely chopped
1/2 cup onion, finely chopped
1/2 pound mushrooms, sliced
2 medium tomatoes, coarsely chopped
1/4 teaspoon cayenne pepper
1 tablespoon sweet pickles, finely chopped
2 tablespoons seedless raisins
6 small stuffed olives, chopped
1 (10-ounce) can mushroom soup
1/2 cup water
3 (8-ounce) rounds of Edam cheese, cut in 1/4-inch slices
1/2 cup freshly grated parmesan cheese

Jan Girando of Leawood, Kansas, doesn't remember the origin of Keshy Yena—and her guests don't care. They are just happy to enjoy this rich, unique dish which makes any meal a celebration!

Combine 1/4 cup flour, salt and 1/4 teaspoon pepper. Dredge beef strips in flour mixture. In heavy sauce pan brown beef strips in 1/2 cup of the butter. Stir in remaining 2 tablespoons flour and cook 1 minute. Stir in wine, cook 2 more minutes. Set aside. In skillet, sauté green pepper, onion and mushrooms in remaining butter. Add tomatoes, cayenne and remaining 1/4 teaspoon pepper; continue cooking until liquid evaporates. Stir in pickles, raisins and olives. In large bowl combine beef and vegetable mixtures. Stir in mushroom soup and water. Line the bottom and sides of a 3-quart casserole dish with slices of cheese. Fill the casserole with the beef/vegetable mixture. Top with parmesan cheese. Bake at 350 degrees for 30 minutes or until the cheese is bubbly. Serve over white rice. Makes 6 servings.

BEEF BURGUNDY

3 tablespoons flour
1 1/2 teaspoons salt
1/2 teaspoon pepper
1/2 teaspoon thyme
3 tablespoons cooking oil, divided
3 pounds stew meat
1 (15-ounce) can beef broth
2 cups burgundy wine
1/2 pound fresh mushrooms
12 small white onions

Preheat oven to 325 degrees. In small bowl combine flour, salt, pepper and thyme. Heat 1 tablespoon oil in heavy skillet over medium heat. Add as much of the meat as pan will hold without crowding. (You will need to divide into 2 or 3 batches.) As juices from meat start to appear, sprinkle with flour mixture and stir well to coat. Continue until all meat is browned, adding more oil as needed. Transfer meat to 4 quart casserole. Pour beef broth and wine over meat. Cover and bake two hours. Add mushrooms and onions. Cover and continue baking for 1 1/2 hours. Makes 8 servings.

BLUE RIBBON MEAT LOAF

1 onion, chopped
1 clove garlic, minced
1 carrot, shredded
1 teaspoon butter, melted
2 pounds ground chuck
1 egg
1 (4-ounce) can whole green chilies, drained and diced
1 (4-ounce) can sliced mushrooms, drained
1/4 teaspoon dried parsley
1/4 teaspoon dill weed
1 teaspoon salt
20 soda crackers, crushed
1 (8-ounce) can tomato sauce, divided

Coat the inside of a loaf pan with cooking spray. Place onion, garlic, carrot and butter in a small microwave-safe dish. Cook for 30 seconds. In a large bowl combine onion mixture, meat, egg, chilies, mushrooms, parsley, dill weed, salt, crackers and half of the tomato sauce. Place mixture in loaf pan. Top with remaining tomato sauce. Bake at 375 degrees for 60 minutes. Makes 8 servings.

Ruby Downing of Oak Grove, Missouri, has made this tasty meat loaf for years and everyone who has tasted it agrees she deserves a blue ribbon! The mushrooms and dill give it that distinctive taste.

JERK PORK TENDERLOIN

4 (12 to 16-ounce) pork tenderloins
Walkerwood jerk seasoning
Olive oil

Mix two tablespoons of jerk seasoning with a tablespoon of olive oil. Rub the tenderloins with the seasoning. Mix additional jerk seasoning if needed. The more you rub on, the spicier your jerk will be. Refrigerate for about an hour. Sear the tenderloins directly over a hot charcoal fire. Move the seared meat away from the coals. Cover the grill and open all vents. Cook 8 to 10 minutes per side. Makes 8 to 10 servings.

KCPTip: *Pork tenderloin for two can be an elegant dinner and is quick to prepare. Melt 2 tablespoons butter in a small heavy skillet. Add a 1-pound tenderloin and brown over high heat for 3 to 4 minutes. Add 2 tablespoons minced shallots and saute for another 2 to 3 minutes. Deglaze with 1/2 cup chicken broth. Reduce heat to low, cover and simmer until done, about 20 to 25 minutes. Turn meat once or twice during cooking process. (For a richer version, substitute 1/2 to 3/4 cup heavy cream for the chicken broth.)*

PORK TENDERLOIN—
SOUTHERN COMFORT STYLE

1 1/2 to 2 pounds pork tenderloin, trimmed

Marinade
1/3 cup olive oil
1/4 cup Southern Comfort
1 clove garlic, finely chopped
1/2 teaspoon dried rosemary
1/4 teaspoon salt
1/4 teaspoon freshly ground black pepper
Grated zest of 1 orange
Juice of 1 orange

In a glass dish combine marinade ingredients. Add meat, turning several times to coat well. Cover and marinate in refrigerator for 2 hours. Preheat oven to 350 degrees. Remove tenderloins from marinade and roast for about 1 hour, basting 5 or 6 times with reserved marinade. (Can also be cooked on outdoor grill over medium-hot fire for about 8 to 10 minutes per side, turning and basting often.) Makes 4 to 6 servings.

"My personal preference for using Southern Comfort in a marinade is the result of a happy accident. I ran out of wine, but had an old bottle of Southern Comfort. I used it and found the result so satisfying that I now prefer using this liqueur (once the favorite of '60s singer Janis Joplin) in place of wine in some of my cooking."
Shifra Stein
Kansas City, Missouri

SLOW SMOKED SPARERIBS

"My advice on cooking ribs: 'Keep the fire low and smoke them slow.'"
Rich Davis Kansas City, Missouri (And he should know! In a town of great rib cooks, Rich is surely one of the best!)

2 slabs of pork spareribs
Dry rub
KC Masterpiece barbecue sauce

Dry Rub
1/2 cup brown sugar
1/2 cup coarsely ground black pepper
1/2 cup paprika
1/4 cup chili powder
1/4 cup salt
2 tablespoons garlic powder

Trim excess fat from ribs. Remove membranes that cover the underside of ribs. Rub the dry rub mix heavily on all sides of the ribs. Cover and marinate for 4 to 24 hours. The flavor from the dry rub will be more pronounced as the marinating time increases.

To cook using a smoker: Prepare smoker with enough coals to last approximately 4 hours. Place water-soaked wood chunks (KC Masterpiece uses hickory wood) on top of coals. The temperature should register 200 to 225 degrees at meat level. Place ribs bone side down with the arch of the ribs at the top. Smoke for approximately 3 to 4 hours rotating the ribs from time to time. Baste with KC Masterpiece barbecue sauce approximately 30 minutes before removing from the smoker. Ribs will be done when the meat has pulled away from the bone.

To cook using a grill: Start charcoal and let coals burn down to white on the outside. Leave the charcoal mounded up on one side of the grill. Place water-soaked hickory chunks on the charcoal. The temperature should register 200 to 225 degrees at meat level. Place ribs bone side down with the arch of the ribs away from the side with the fire. Close the lid on the grill leaving any vents slightly open. Cook for 3 to 4 hours, rotating ribs from time to time. Baste with KC Masterpiece barbecue sauce approximately 30 minutes before removing from the grill. Ribs will be done when the meat has pulled away from the bone.

PORK PICCATA

1-pound pork tenderloin, sliced thin and flattened
1 teaspoon salt
1/8 teaspoon pepper
2 eggs, well beaten
1 1/4 cups butter, divided
1 (8-ounce) package spaghetti, cooked and drained
3/4 cup shredded Swiss cheese
1/4 cup finely chopped chives

Season tenderloin slices with salt and pepper, dip in beaten egg and sauté in 1/4 cup butter. In small pan brown remaining butter until dark and pour over spaghetti. To serve place spaghetti on a hot platter. Arrange tenderloin slices over spaghetti; sprinkle with cheese and chives. Makes 4 servings.

KCPT *ip: To reduce fat content, brown tenderloin in nonstick pan with cooking spray. You can also eliminate the egg dip, or reduce the amount of butter that is browned and poured over the spaghetti.*

"My father-in-law, Bill Vandenberg, Sr., was a ticket agent at Union Station from 1941 to 1978. He got this recipe from the chef at The Westport Room. It's still a family favorite."
Mariann Herndon Vandenberg Overland Park, Kansas

BAKED PORK CHOPS

2 tablespoons cooking oil
4 thick boneless pork chops
3/4 cup catsup
1/2 cup wine vinegar
1 teaspoon cinnamon
1 bay leaf, broken into large pieces

In heavy skillet brown pork chops on both sides in hot oil; transfer to baking dish. Combine catsup, vinegar, cinnamon and bay leaf. Stir to blend well. Pour over pork chops. Cover tightly and bake for 1 hour at 350 degrees or until chops are tender. Makes 4 servings.

KC STYLE CHOUCROUTE GARNI

When the weather turns cold, Lou Jane Temple, Kansas City, Missouri, likes to make this deluxe one-pot sauerkraut dish using locally smoked meats and sausages. She served it to a gathering of Kansas City food critics— and garnered rave reviews.

2 pounds deli sauerkraut, drained
2 tablespoons juniper berries
2 tablespoons caraway seeds
1 cup dry white wine
1 cup chicken broth or stock
8 large (8-ounce or larger) smoked pork chops
3 smoked ham hocks
4 large or 8 small bratwurst
1 pound smoked or Polish sausage

Preheat oven to 350 degrees. In a large roasting pan place the sauerkraut, juniper berries, caraway seeds, wine and chicken broth. Stir to blend. Arrange the pork chops, ham hocks, and sausages over the sauerkraut. Put the lid on the roaster and roast in the oven for 1 hour. Check occasionally and add more wine and broth if necessary. Serve hot; pass coarsely ground mustard and freshly grated horseradish. Makes 8 servings.

GRILLED LEG OF LAMB

1 (7-pound) leg of lamb, butterflied by your butcher
1 cup veal or chicken stock
Salt and pepper to taste

Marinade
1/2 cup Zinfandel
1/4 cup brandy
1/4 cup soy sauce
Juice of 1 medium orange
Juice of 1 lemon
1 teaspoon dry mustard
1 large tomato, chopped
3 cloves garlic, minced
1/4 teaspoon freshly ground black pepper
2 tablespoons honey

Open leg of lamb so it is flat; pound meat so it is of uniform thickness. Combine wine, brandy, soy sauce, orange juice, lemon juice, mustard, tomato, garlic, pepper and honey in blender or food processor; process 15 seconds. Place lamb in a heavy plastic bag with a zip-lock top, pour marinade over, turn to coat. Place in refrigerator and marinate 8 to 12 hours or overnight, turning occasionally. Prepare grill for high heat grilling. Remove lamb from marinade; reserve 1/2 cup of liquid. Place lamb on grill 3 inches from flame. Grill each side 15 to 20 minutes for medium-rare to medium or to your preference. Remove to platter and let rest 5 minutes. Meanwhile, in medium saucepan combine reserved marinade with stock. Bring to a boil and reduce to 3/4 cup. Taste for seasoning. To serve, spoon sauce onto hot plates. Slice lamb across the grain and place on top of sauce. Makes 6 to 8 servings.

"The original recipe is one I got from a winery in Napa Valley. It's become a standard in my barbecue repertoire. As a side dish, I often prepare Two Cheese Potatoes (page 45). A nice Cabernet is the perfect complement."
Joseph J. Roh
Leawood, Kansas

RICH'S GRILLED MARINATED CHICKEN

"It's the long marinating time that gives this chicken its piquant taste. Cook extra boneless breasts and slice for a delicious next-day chicken salad."
Rich Davis
Kansas City, Missouri

1 (3-pound) chicken, cut in pieces, or boneless chicken
  breasts

Marinade
3 cups water
1 tablespoon orange juice concentrate
2 teaspoons lemon juice
3/4 cup minced onion
2 teaspoons granulated garlic
2 teaspoons thyme
1/2 teaspoon rosemary
1 teaspoon sage
1 tablespoon celery salt
1 1/2 tablespoons salt
2 teaspoons black pepper

Combine marinade ingredients in a large jar with a screw-top lid and shake well to blend. Place chicken in heavy plastic bag with zip-lock top, pour marinade over chicken, covering well. Let sit in refrigerator, turning occasionally, for 8 to 24 hours. Grill over hot fire until done, turning often. Makes 3 to 4 servings.

LIME-GARLIC CHICKEN

1 (3 to 3 1/2-pound) frying chicken, cut in pieces, or split in half, or whole for roasting

Marinade
Juice of 6 limes
5 cloves of garlic, finely minced
2 tablespoons sesame oil
4 teaspoons fresh rosemary

Combine marinade ingredients in a large jar with a screw-top lid and shake well to blend. Place chicken in heavy plastic bag with zip-lock top, pour marinade over chicken, covering well. Let sit in refrigerator, turning occasionally, for 2 to 4 hours. Remove chicken from bag, reserve marinade. Grill chicken over a hot fire, roast or cook on rotisserie, basting occasionally with reserved marinade. Makes 3 to 4 servings.

KCPT *ip:* *When you're grilling, prepare extra chicken breasts and enjoy deluxe sandwiches the next day, using Joy's recipe for Caesar Sauce. Combine 1/4 cup plus 1 tablespoon mayonnaise; 1/4 cup plus 2 tablespoons grated parmesan cheese; 3 anchovy filets, finely chopped; 1 clove garlic, minced; 1 teaspoon dijon mustard; 1 tablespoon lemon juice; salt and pepper to taste. Sauce generously on sandwich buns, top with chicken and lettuce leaves. Makes 4 servings.*

"This is a favorite dish for summertime entertaining. It can be cooked in an indoor oven but it's better outside— especially good when cooked on the rotisserie."
Marty Morris
Blue Springs, Missouri

CHICKEN MACIEL

"Joe Maciel, popular host at the famous Fred Harvey Westport Room at the Kansas City Union Station, personally invented this dish, which became one of the most asked for on the menu. The recipe was shared with Bill Vandenberg, Sr., in the 1950s and is still served frequently in the Vandenberg household."
Mariann Herndon Vandenberg Overland Park, Kansas

1/4 cup butter
3 cups cooked white meat of chicken, in 1-inch cubes
2 teaspoons curry powder
1/4 cup sherry
2 cups cooked rice
4 cups hot cream sauce
Salt to taste
White pepper to taste
1 cup shredded Swiss cheese

In heavy skillet sauté chicken in melted butter with curry powder and sherry. In a large bowl fold chicken and rice into cream sauce and stir carefully until blended. Season to taste. Place in individual casseroles, or one 3-quart casserole; sprinkle with cheese. Place casseroles under broiler until top is brown. Makes 6 servings.

KCPT *ip:To make about a cup of white sauce: In a small saucepan melt 2 tablespoons butter over low heat; blend in 2 tablespoons flour to form a smooth paste. Gradually whisk in 1 cup of milk and heat, stirring constantly, until thickened and smooth. Add 1/4 teaspoon salt and a pinch of pepper. Continue to cook about 5 minutes over low heat, stirring occasionally.*

GARLIC LOVER'S CHICKEN ROMANO

3/4 cup olive oil, divided
1 head garlic
1 cup dry bread crumbs
1/2 cup grated romano cheese
1/4 cup chopped parsley
Salt and pepper to taste
4 chicken breasts, split, skinned and boned

In blender blend 1/2 cup oil and garlic. Place in bowl and set aside. In a large bowl combine the bread crumbs, cheese, parsley, salt and pepper. Dip each breast in oil mixture then coat with bread crumb mixture. In a heavy skillet fry the chicken in remaining oil until golden brown, about 5 minutes per side. Place in a 9 x 13-inch baking pan and bake at 350 for 30 minutes. Makes 6 to 8 servings.

TARRAGON CHICKEN

2 teaspoons canola oil
Seasoned flour for dredging
4 boneless, skinless chicken breast halves
1 cup white wine
1 cup chicken stock
4 tablespoons fresh tarragon, chopped
2 tablespoons fresh chervil, chopped
2 carrots, peeled and cut into 1-inch chunks
2 ribs celery, cut into 1-inch chunks

In a heavy skillet, heat oil over medium-high heat until hot. Dredge chicken breasts in flour and cook in oil until brown on both sides. Add wine, chicken stock, tarragon and chervil. Bring to a boil; reduce heat, cover and simmer for 15 minutes. Add vegetables and baste the meat with the cooking liquid. Cover and continue to cook for another 15 minutes, until done. Remove meat and vegetables to a serving platter. The cooking liquid should have reduced to the consistency of a sauce during the cooking process. If it has not, raise the heat and reduce. Makes 4 servings.

CUBAN STYLE FRIED CHICKEN

1 (3 to 4-pound) frying chicken, cut into pieces, washed and drained
Juice of 2 lemons
10 cloves garlic, minced
3 tablespoons salt, divided
2 1/2 teaspoons black pepper, divided
3 cups flour
4 tablespoons granulated garlic
1 1/2 quarts vegetable, canola or olive oil

Place chicken in large stainless steel or porcelain bowl. Season with lemon juice, garlic, 1 tablespoon of the salt and 1 teaspoon of the pepper. Toss well, cover and refrigerate for 2 to 4 hours, turning occasionally. In a paper or plastic bag combine flour, granulated garlic and remaining salt and pepper. Shake well to mix. Place chicken in the flour mixture and dredge evenly. In a deep heavy pan heat the oil to 350 degrees. Cook chicken in the hot oil, in batches of 3 to 4 pieces, turning when halfway cooked. Cook until chicken starts to float, approximately 10 minutes. Place chicken on a paper towel to drain. Transfer to baking sheet and place in 300 degree oven for 10 to 15 minutes to drain extra oil. Makes 3 to 4 servings.

CHICKEN MARANGO

10 to 12 slices of bacon
8 boneless, skinless chicken breasts
Seasoned flour for dredging
2 medium onions, chopped
2 to 3 cloves of garlic, minced
1 (15-ounce) can diced tomatoes, with juice
1 (8-ounce) can whole button mushrooms, drained,
  liquid reserved
1/4 cup chopped parsley, divided

In a large sauté pan fry bacon until crisp. Remove bacon to drain on paper towels; keep bacon grease in pan. Crumble bacon when drained. Dredge chicken breasts in flour to coat; save remaining flour. Brown chicken breasts in bacon grease. Place in a 9 x 13-inch baking dish. Pour off half of the remaining grease. Sauté chopped onion in grease until soft. Add minced garlic and remaining flour; stir to form a roux. Add tomatoes, mushrooms, half the parsley and half the bacon. Heat to boiling, stirring constantly. If tomato gravy is too thick, thin with reserved mushroom liquid. Pour gravy over chicken and top with remaining bacon. Bake at 350 degrees for approximately 1 hour. Sprinkle remaining parsley over chicken and serve. Makes 8 servings.

KEPT *ip: Tomato gravy can be made ahead and refrigerated or frozen. Chicken could then be sautéed in oil.*

"This is a wonderful 'company's coming' casserole that can be prepared ahead. Easy to double, too."
Judi Walker
Lawrence, Kansas

CHARLES' QUAIL CASSEROLE

"It's hard to spoil a quail. But a taste of this will cause a wife to forgive her truant husband for spending the whole autumn in the field."
C. W. Gusewelle
Kansas City,
Missouri

Seasoned flour for dredging
2 tablespoons vegetable oil
8 quail, split in half, backbone removed
2 (10-ounce) cans cream of mushroom soup
1 (10-ounce) can cream of celery soup
1 1/2 cups dry white wine
1 large can ready-to-bake biscuits

Preheat oven to 400 degrees. Dredge quail halves in flour. In heavy skillet brown quail lightly in hot oil. Remove quail to 3-quart casserole dish. Pour soups over quail; add wine. Tear biscuits into halves and place over top, covering quail completely. Cover and bake about 1 hour, or until breasts are tender. Uncover and continue baking until biscuit tops are browned, about 10 minutes. Makes 4 servings.

QUAIL ON A BED OF LEEKS

This recipe also works well with boneless chicken breasts.

4 slices bacon
Seasoned flour for dredging
6 quail, split in half, breast bone removed
1/4 cup butter
2 leeks, cleaned and chopped
10 ounces button mushrooms
1/2 teaspoon dried oregano
1 cup dry white wine
2 tablespoons lemon juice
1/2 cup chicken broth

Preheat oven to 350 degrees. In a heavy skillet, cook bacon until crisp. Drain on paper towels; leave drippings in pan. Dredge quail halves in seasoned flour and sauté in bacon drippings over medium-high heat until browned, about 2 to 3 minutes each side. Remove from skillet and place on paper towels. Pour off bacon drippings. In same skillet sauté leeks in butter for 2 minutes. Crumble bacon and add to skillet along with mushrooms and oregano and cook for 2 more minutes. Spoon the leek mixture into a 3-quart casserole. Place the quail on top of the leeks. Pour the wine, lemon juice and broth over the quail. Bake for 1 hour. Serve hot with saffron rice. Makes 4 servings.

DUCK BREAST
WITH RED WINE DEMI-GLACÉ

2 duck breasts, split
4 tablespoons seasoned flour
2 tablespoons oil
3/4 cup red wine
2 tablespoons butter

Lightly dust duck breasts with seasoned flour. In a large pan sauté duck breasts in oil for about 4 to 5 minutes per side until lightly browned. Remove duck from pan and arrange on plates. Immediately add red wine to pan and reduce by half over high heat. Add butter; pour sauce over duck and serve. Makes 4 servings.

GRILLED VENISON MEDALLIONS
WITH GARLIC AND CAPERS

4 to 8 venison medallions or chops
2 tablespoons olive oil
2 cloves garlic, minced
2 tablespoons capers
3/4 cup dry white wine
2 tablespoons butter

For marinade, combine oil, garlic, capers and wine. Place venison in a shallow glass dish and cover with marinade. Cover and refrigerate for 1 hour. Reserving the marinade, grill venison over hot charcoal (or high flame on a gas grill) until just browned, about 2 to 3 minutes per side. Venison is very lean; overcooking will produce tough meat. Place meat on a platter and keep warm. In a small saucepan bring marinade to a boil; add butter and stir until melted. Pour sauce over medallions. Makes 4 servings.

"My husband Dick is a hunter and my first lessons in cooking were with game. I hunt occasionally too, enjoying the day in the fields with usually very little to show for it!"
Karen Adler
Kansas City, Missouri

To use this recipe with chicken breasts, increase grill time to 5 to 7 minutes per side.

TWO-HOUR TURKEY

"This recipe sounds
unusual—it is and
very good! It's the
only way I fix
turkey now. I
learned the
technique in
Atlanta, Georgia,
when I took
cooking lessons
from a wonderful
chef named Ursula.
One of her trade-
mark sayings was
'You are the boss
in your kitchen.'"
Joyce Kemp
Shawnee Mission,
Kansas

1 tablespoon oil
1 (10 to 12-pound) turkey, giblets and neck removed
1 teaspoon lemon pepper
2 teaspoons salt
1 medium onion
1/2 cup parsley stems
1 teaspoon rosemary
1 carrot, cut in 1-inch chunks
1 rib celery, cut in 1-inch chunks
1 large onion, quartered
1/2 cup cognac or brandy
1 cup white wine
1 (15-ounce) can chicken broth
1/2 cup tomato or mixed vegetable juice

Gravy
1 tablespoon cornstarch
3 tablespoons whipping cream
1 teaspoon Kitchen Bouquet

Preheat oven to 425 degrees. Line a shallow baking pan with doubled heavy-duty foil so shiny side of foil is up. Edges of foil should extend well beyond end of baking pan. Spray foil with cooking spray and grease with oil. Rinse the turkey and dry. Sprinkle lemon pepper and salt in cavity and under neck skin. Put onion under neck skin; fold wings under back to hold neck skin under wings. Do not salt the skin. Put parsley stems and rosemary in cavity. Tie legs together loosely. Place turkey on the foil. Place carrot, celery and onion around the turkey. (Note: Recipe can be prepared to this point ahead of time and refrigerated. Let sit at room temperature for 1 hour before cooking.)

In small pan heat cognac and wine. Do not boil. Pour half of the liquid into the cavity and the other half over the turkey. Combine the chicken broth and tomato juice; heat and pour over and around the turkey. Form a large tent for the turkey out of 2 long sheets of heavy-duty foil. Place the tent over the turkey completely sealing the edges of the foil around the pan. Do not let foil touch the top of the turkey. The key to the turkey being done in two hours is that, for the first hour, the bird is sealed airtight. Bake for 1 hour on lowest rack of oven.

Remove from oven. Cut foil tent lengthwise and push to sides. Be careful of escaping steam. Reduce heat to 400 degrees and bake, uncovered, for 1 hour longer. Do not baste. When turkey is done, remove from pan and place on serving tray. Pour pan juices into saucepan; remove excess grease. Bring the juice to a boil. In a jar with a tight-fitting lid combine cornstarch, whipping cream and Kitchen Bouquet. Shake to mix well. Add to drippings; stir to thicken. Makes 8 to 10 servings.

KCPT *ip: Give your leftover turkey a whole new persona with Diane Hogerty's recipe for Curry Casserole. Butter a 2 quart casserole dish. In it place 1 1/2 to 2 cups cooked chopped turkey, top with 2 cups fresh broccoli, blanched for 2 minutes.*

Combine 1 can cream of chicken soup, 1/2 cup mayonnaise, 1/2 teaspoon lemon juice, and 1/2 teaspoon curry powder. Pour mixture over chicken and broccoli. Top with 1/2 cup grated sharp cheddar cheese and 1/2 cup bread crumbs that have been mixed with 2 tablespoons melted butter. Bake at 350 degrees for one hour.

BAKED SHRIMP STUFFED WITH SUN-DRIED TOMATOES AND WHITE WINE

1 (6-ounce) box herb stuffing mix
3/4 cup diced celery
1/4 cup oil-packed sun-dried tomatoes, drained and diced
1 (6-ounce) can crab meat
1 (8-ounce) package cream cheese
1/2 teaspoon Italian seasoning
1 clove garlic, minced
1/2 cup white wine, divided
20 jumbo shrimp, cleaned and butterflied
2 tablespoons butter, in small pieces
Cracked black pepper

Preheat oven to 350 degrees. Prepare stuffing according to package directions, adding diced celery and sun-dried tomatoes to water just before adding bread crumbs. In a small bowl combine crab meat, cream cheese, seasoning, garlic and 1/4 cup white wine. Add to stuffing; mix well. On an ungreased baking sheet, place golf ball-sized ball of stuffing/cheese mixture. Place a butterflied shrimp over the stuffing. Continue with remaining stuffing/cheese mixture and shrimp. Put the butter pieces in the pan and drizzle with remaining white wine and pepper. Bake 20 to 30 minutes, until the shrimp are cooked through. Makes 10 servings.

WILD RICE, SHRIMP AND MUSHROOM CASSEROLE

8 ounces fresh mushrooms, sliced
6 tablespoons butter, divided
1/4 cup flour
2 cups milk
1 (8-ounce) package cream cheese, at room temperature
2 (6-ounce) packages long grain and wild rice, prepared
2 (4-ounce) cans tiny shrimp, drained
1 pound fresh or 2 (10-ounce) packages frozen asparagus
   spears, steamed

In small pan sauté mushrooms in 2 tablespoons of the butter 5 to 6 minutes; set aside. In a medium pan melt remaining butter. Stir in flour to form a smooth paste. Gradually stir in milk and heat, stirring occasionally, until thickened and smooth. Add cream cheese and stir until melted. Stir in mushrooms. In a large bowl combine rice and shrimp, stirring lightly to combine. To serve, place 5 to 6 asparagus spears on each plate. Add a layer of rice and shrimp mixture and top with a generous dollop of the mushroom sauce. Makes 6 to 8 servings.

"My son Daniel, now a student at Duke University, has loved this dish since he was a little boy. He suggested I send it in."
Nancy Swanwick
Fort Scott, Kansas

MICROWAVED SHRIMP IN SHELL

3 pounds fresh shrimp in shell
Onion powder
Garlic powder
Red pepper flakes
Cinnamon
Old Bay spice mix
3 tablespoons water

Place a layer of shrimp around the outer edge of a round, 3-quart microwave-safe bowl. Sprinkle spices over layer. Place another layer of shrimp on top; do not fill in the center of bowl. Sprinkle spices over layer. Continue with layers until all shrimp are used. Put water in the center of bowl; cover lightly. Microwave on high for 4 minutes. Makes 4 to 6 servings.

"My son Buzz and I wanted some shrimp, but not fried or boiled. So we concocted this recipe. We tried various other spices, but this combination tastes the best."
"Coop" Cooper
Kansas City, Missouri

MARY ANN'S CAJUN-STYLE SHRIMP

"One of my favorite. Be sure to serve along with individual rolls of paper towels— wonderfully messy! (To double the recipe make a fresh batch.)"
Mary Ann Reed
Kansas City, Missouri

1 cup (2 sticks) butter
1 cup vegetable oil
2 teaspoons finely minced garlic
4 bay leaves, crushed
2 tablespoons crushed dried rosemary leaves
1/2 teaspoon dried basil
1/2 teaspoon oregano
1/2 teaspoon salt
1/2 teaspoon cayenne pepper
1 tablespoon paprika
3/4 teaspoon ground pepper
1 tablespoon fresh lemon juice
2 pounds fresh shrimp in shell

Melt butter in heavy saucepan; add oil and mix well. Add all remaining ingredients except shrimp. Cook over medium heat, stirring constantly until sauce begins to boil. Reduce heat; simmer 7 to 8 minutes, stirring frequently. Remove from heat. Let stand uncovered at room temperature for 30 minutes. Add shrimp to sauce, mix thoroughly. Cook over medium heat 6 to 8 minutes or until shrimp turns pink. Place in a baking dish and bake at 450 degrees for ten minutes. To serve, place shrimp in individual bowls, ladle 1/2 cup sauce over shrimp. Makes 4 servings.

BAKED CATFISH

1 whole catfish, about 1 pound
2 tablespoons canola oil
1 small onion, diced
1 tablespoon flour
Salt to taste
1 (15-ounce) can diced tomatoes
1 clove garlic, minced
1/2 teaspoon thyme

Wash fish in cold water; pat with salt and let stand for a few minutes. Wash again and dry with a paper towel. In a medium pan sauté onion in oil; add flour and salt to taste. When mixture is dry and slightly brown, add tomatoes, garlic and thyme. Stir to mix; cook 5 minutes. Place fish in a baking dish; pour sauce over fish. Bake at 350 degrees for 45 minutes, basting every 10 minutes. Fish is done when white puffs begin to show. Makes 2 servings.

KCPT *ip: Shirin Khodayari offers an alternate method for preparing baked fish. Combine 1/4 cup olive oil; 1 clove garlic, minced; 1 teaspoon fresh crushed rosemary; juice of 1/2 fresh lime and 1 teaspoon seafood seasoning. Pour over catfish and top with 1 small white onion, sliced in wedges. Cover and refrigerate for one hour. Heat 2 tablespoons olive oil in skillet and sauté fish on both sides. Return to baking dish, add 1 can diced tomatoes and bake at 350 degrees for around 20 minutes. Then broil (or grill) for about 10 minutes or until flaky and done.*

"This recipe came from Bertha Draskowich who got it from Annie Loncaric. Annie immigrated to the Strawberry Hill area around 1925. She came from Yugoslavia where she lived near the Adriatic Sea. The recipe can also be used for salmon."
Anthony Pickert
Overland Park, Kansas

SALMON STEAKS
WITH APPLE MARINADE

4 salmon steaks, about 1-inch thick

Marinade
1/2 cup apple juice
1/3 cup soy sauce
2 cloves garlic, minced
2 tablespoons butter

In a medium pan combine apple juice, soy sauce and garlic. Boil until mixture coats spoon, about 3 to 5 minutes. Add butter; cook another minute. Allow to cool. Place salmon in a glass dish and pour marinade over, turning to coat. Cover and marinate at room temperature for 30 minutes or in refrigerator for 2 hours. Place fish on greased broiler pan. Broil 4 inches from heat for about 5 minutes, basting once with marinade. Turn fish; brush with marinade and broil 4 to 6 minutes more until fish flakes easily with fork. Discard remaining marinade. Makes 4 servings.

KCPT *ip: Try Ed Scanlon's Sauce Verte with smoked or grilled salmon. It's from his family's cookbook. Combine the following: 1 cup mayonnaise, 1/2 cup fresh chopped parsley, 1 tablespoon tarragon vinegar, 1/3 cup fresh chopped dill, 2 tablespoons capers, and 1 tablespoon fresh chopped chives. Process in blender until smooth. Refrigerate for at least one hour to blend flavors.*

FAST FISH, ENGLISH PUB STYLE

1/2 cup flour
1/2 cup flat English ale or beer
1 tablespoon malt vinegar
1/2 teaspoon baking soda
Salt and pepper to taste
Vegetable oil (for frying)
1 (12-ounce) cod or orange roughy fillet, 1/2-inch thick,
　　cut crosswise into 8 strips

In a medium bowl combine flour, ale, vinegar and baking soda with a whisk until well blended. Season batter generously with salt and pepper. Pour oil into heavy skillet to depth of 1/2 inch. Heat oil to 350 degrees. Pat fish dry with paper towels; season with salt and pepper. Dip 4 strips into batter; let excess batter drain back into bowl. Fry fish in hot oil until brown on both sides and just cooked through, about 3 minutes per side. Using slotted spoon, transfer fish to paper towels and let drain. Repeat with remaining fish strips. Arrange fish on platter. Serve, passing additional malt vinegar separately. Makes 2 servings.

Fish and chips is a popular dish in many English pubs and takeaways. Now Jane Wagner, Kansas City, Missouri, shares her recipe which is a hit with all her pals. Serve with fresh, crispy French fries.

BAKED STUFFED RIGATONI

"I adapted this from a recipe I found in a magazine and my family loves it! It will seem like too much sauce but pile it on (use a deep baking dish). And be sure to stuff the rigatoni or they'll squirt sauce all over the oven!"
Kathy Smith
Shawnee, Kansas

3 tablespoons olive oil
1 1/2 pounds ground beef
1 small onion, chopped
1 clove garlic, minced
3 (6-ounce) cans tomato paste
9 cups water
1/3 cup sugar
1 1/2 teaspoons oregano
1 bay leaf
1/2 teaspoon red pepper
2 teaspoons fennel seeds
1 1/2 teaspoons salt
1 (16-ounce) package rigatoni
Grated parmesan or romano cheese

In a heavy saucepan brown meat in hot oil along with onion and garlic. Cook, stirring frequently, until meat is completely brown. Remove about half to use for stuffing pasta. To remaining meat mixture add tomato paste, water, sugar, oregano, bay leaf, pepper, fennel and salt. Bring to a boil; reduce heat and simmer for 1 hour. Meanwhile, cook pasta in boiling salted water until firmly tender, 12 to 15 minutes. Drain, and when cool enough to handle, stuff pieces of pasta with the reserved meat. Place layer of stuffed pasta in bottom of 3-quart casserole. Cover with layer of sauce. Repeat until all the pasta and sauce are used, finishing with a layer of sauce. Sprinkle generously with cheese. Bake at 350 degrees for 40 minutes or until heated through and cheese is lightly browned. Makes 6 to 8 servings.

SLUMGULLION

1 pound ground beef
1/2 large green pepper, chopped
1/2 large onion, chopped
1 (28-ounce) can crushed tomatoes
1 teaspoon worcestershire sauce
1 cup spicy tomato juice
1 teaspoon Italian seasoning
Salt and pepper to taste
1 (8-ounce) package elbow macaroni, cooked and
  drained
1 cup shredded cheddar cheese

In a heavy skillet brown beef with pepper and onion; drain. Add tomatoes, worcestershire sauce, juice, Italian seasoning, salt and pepper to beef mixture. Stir to combine. Mix tomato and meat mixture with cooked macaroni and place in 9 x 13-inch baking dish. Top with cheese and bake at 325 degrees for 45 minutes. Makes 6 to 8 servings.

KEPT *ip: Variations: add 2 cups sliced mushrooms before baking. Add 1 cup chopped celery when browning meat. Substitute ground pork or sausage for part of the ground beef. Add 1/2 teaspoon chili powder with other seasonings. Substitute monterey jack pepper cheese for the cheddar.*

Dee Conde of Kansas City, Missouri, made "Slumgullion" often when her children were young. There are many versions of this ever popular dish. Sally Quinn, who calls hers "Johnny Marzetti," has been known to serve it to gatherings of the Washington D.C. political elite!

POLENTA TERESE

1 1/2 pounds lean ground beef
1 medium onion, chopped
3 to 4 green onions, sliced
1 medium green bell pepper, chopped
1 (8-ounce) can tomato sauce
1/4 teaspoon paprika
1/4 teaspoon garlic powder
1 teaspoon chili powder
1 (8 1/2-ounce) box corn muffin mix
1 egg
1/3 cup milk
1 teaspoon sugar
1 (15-ounce) can cream style corn

Preheat oven to 375 degrees. In a skillet brown the ground beef over medium heat along with the onion, green onion and green pepper. When meat is completely brown, add tomato sauce, paprika, garlic powder and chili powder. Stir to mix and cook 2 to 3 minutes more. Remove from heat and allow to cool slightly. Meanwhile, in a large bowl combine the corn muffin mix, egg, milk, sugar and corn. Stir to mix well. Pour half of the batter into a greased 2 1/2-quart shallow casserole. Spread the meat mixture evenly over the batter, then top with the remaining batter. The batter should cover the meat as completely as possible. Bake at 375 degrees for 40 to 45 minutes until lightly browned and bubbly. Makes 6 servings.

ENCHILADAS

1 pound ground beef
1/4 cup chopped onion
1/2 teaspoon salt
1 small can enchilada sauce
1 dozen flour tortillas
2 tablespoons butter
2 tablespoons flour
2/3 cup chicken broth
2 tablespoons chopped green pepper
1/2 cup sour cream
1 cup shredded cheddar cheese

In a heavy skillet brown beef along with onion; drain. Add salt and enchilada sauce; stir to mix. Spoon approximately 3 tablespoons meat mixture onto each tortilla; sprinkle with 1 tablespoon cheddar cheese and roll up. Place seam side down in a 9 x 13-inch baking dish. In a saucepan melt butter; blend in flour, then broth. Cook over medium heat until thickened. Gradually stir in green pepper and sour cream. Pour mixture over tortillas and sprinkle remaining cheese over top. Bake at 350 until heated, approximately 15 minutes. Makes 6 servings.

"Anytime I take this dish to a get-together, people always ask for the recipe, which is one my mother gave me. It's also very good made with chicken. Substitute cooked, cubed chicken for the hamburger."
Debby Burkhardt
Independence, Missouri

BONNIE'S RED BEANS AND RICE

Bonnie Jones of Independence, Missouri, has lived and cooked around the world. She even has a letter of commendation from the Marines thanking her for preparing such good food for a Marine unit in Germany!

1 (16-ounce) bag dried small red beans
2 large smoked ham hocks
10 cups water
2 1/2 cups finely chopped celery
2 cups finely chopped onion
2 cups finely chopped green bell pepper
5 whole bay leaves
2 teaspoons ground white pepper
2 teaspoons dried thyme
1 1/2 teaspoons garlic powder
1 1/2 teaspoons dried oregano
1 teaspoon cayenne pepper
1/2 teaspoon ground black pepper
1 tablespoon hot pepper sauce
8 ounces smoked pork sausage, cut in half lengthwise, then into 1/8-inch slices
2 cups white rice, cooked according to package directions

Sort and rinse beans, cover with water, soak overnight. In large soup pot, place ham hocks, water, celery, onion, pepper, bay leaves and seasonings. Stir well; bring to boil over high heat. Reduce heat and simmer until meat is tender, about 2 hours, stirring occasionally. Remove ham hocks and set aside. Drain beans and add to pot. Bring to boil; reduce heat and simmer one hour. Debone and defat the ham hocks. Slice the meat thin or shred and return to the soup pot with the pork sausage. Continue simmering, uncovered and stirring often, an hour or more until beans start breaking up and are very tender. Serve with the cooked rice. Makes 12 to 16 servings.

PASTA WITH SMOKED TURKEY AND CILANTRO PESTO

Cilantro Pesto
2 cups fresh cilantro
3 large cloves garlic
1/2 cup chopped walnuts
1/2 teaspoon salt
1/2 cup parmesan cheese
2/3 to 3/4 cup olive oil

3 tablespoons olive oil
2 green bell peppers, cut into strips
1 red bell pepper, cut into strips
1 yellow bell pepper, cut into strips
1/2 cup sliced green onions
2 pounds smoked, fully-cooked turkey breast, cut into
  strips
1 (16-ounce) package fettuccini, cooked and drained

For pesto, place cilantro, garlic, walnuts, salt and cheese in food processor bowl. Process until smooth. Pour oil through chute in a steady stream, processing until mixture is well blended. Set aside. In large pan sauté peppers and green onions in olive oil over medium heat until vegetables are crisp-tender. Add turkey and cook about 5 minutes to heat through. Remove from heat and toss with pasta. Pour pesto over pasta; toss gently to coat well. Makes 8 servings.

"This is a recipe I developed years ago. It's a wonderful entree—one of my favorites for entertaining. You can substitute fresh basil for the cilantro. Without the turkey, it is a very good vegetarian dish."
Roxanne Wyss
Olathe, Kansas

FRAN'S PASTA PIZZETTE

"My sister-in-law, Fran George, created this recipe and shared it with me years ago. I serve it as a main dish with garlic bread. Or if you're a meat lover, serve with grilled Italian sausage."
Karen Merry
Shawnee, Kansas

1 teaspoon butter
1/2 cup pine nuts
1/2 cup olive oil
3 cloves garlic, crushed
1 (16-ounce) can artichoke hearts in brine, cut in eighths
1 (16-ounce) can large pitted black olives, cut in half
1 (16-ounce) package shell pasta, cooked al dente and drained
1 (15-ounce) can baby peas, drained
Grated romano or parmesan cheese

In small pan lightly toast pine nuts in butter over medium heat; set aside. In a large pan sauté garlic in olive oil. Add artichoke hearts, pine nuts and olives. Simmer about 5 minutes. Add pasta; stir lightly to combine. Add peas, stir to combine. Top with cheese. Makes 4 servings.

MARCI'S GREEK PASTA

"This is a 'I don't feel like going to the store, what's in the cupboard that I can throw together' kind of dish! You can add cubed, cooked chicken breast. If you can't find flavored feta, use plain and add basil."
Marci Pickard
Kansas City, Missouri

2 tablespoons olive oil, basil-flavored if desired
1 clove garlic, minced
2 plum tomatoes, chopped
4 green onions, chopped
1 (4-ounce) package tomato-basil flavored feta cheese crumbles
1 (16-ounce) package pasta, cooked and drained
1 (4-ounce) small can pitted ripe olives, drained

In a medium pan sauté garlic, tomatoes and onion in oil. Add cheese, pasta and olives; toss to mix. Makes 4 servings.

PENNE WITH ROASTED TOMATO SAUCE

12 ripe plum tomatoes, cut in half lengthwise and seeded
8 large cloves garlic, sliced very thin
Salt and ground black pepper to taste
4 tablespoons extra virgin olive oil
3 tablespoons dried minced parsley
1 teaspoon dried basil
1/4 teaspoon crushed red pepper
12 ounces penne pasta or other favorite pasta, cooked
   al dente and drained
3 ounces freshly grated parmesan cheese

In a glass baking dish arrange tomatoes with cut sides up. Sprinkle tomatoes with slices of garlic, salt and pepper. Drizzle with olive oil. Bake uncovered at 325 degrees for 2 hours, or until tomatoes have begun to caramelize. Remove from oven and add the parsley, basil and red pepper. Using a knife and fork, cut tomatoes into bite-sized pieces and stir to mix with herbs and seasonings. Place pasta in a large serving bowl. Pour sauce over and toss. Top with parmesan cheese and serve.

Georgia Kuehn, Raytown, Missouri, says she could spend all her time in the kitchen and her co-workers often ask why she doesn't open a restaurant! Ginger's father was an influence on her cooking because he encouraged her to experiment and try new recipes.

PASTA AND BROCCOLI RABE

2 to 4 tablespoons olive oil
2 cloves garlic, chopped
1 to 2 dashes of dried hot peppers
3 to 4 anchovies, chopped
2 bunches broccoli rabe
1 (16-ounce) package spaghetti, cooked al dente and
   drained
Parmesan cheese

In a large pan sauté chopped garlic, peppers and anchovies in olive oil over low heat. In another pan parboil rabe for 2 minutes; chop. Add rabe to oil; sauté for 1 minute. Add spaghetti; toss to mix. Top with parmesan cheese. Serve while hot. Makes 4 servings.

"A friend in Florida prepared this and shared her recipe. You can use broccoli—but the distinctive flavor of the broccoli rabe is what makes it special." Lindsay Major Shawnee Mission, Kansas

TERRESSA'S TUNA NOODLE CASSEROLE

Terressa McGee, Kansas City, Missouri, finds this to be just the right dish for a potluck after church on Sunday or for a relaxing Friday night after the work week.

1/2 pound egg noodles, cooked according to package directions and drained
1 (10-ounce) can cream of mushroom soup
1/2 cup milk
1 (4-ounce) can sliced mushrooms, drained
1 small onion, peeled and chopped
1/4 cup diced pimento
1/4 cup diced green bell pepper
1 3/4 cups shredded sharp cheddar cheese plus 1 cup more to garnish
2 (6-ounce) cans tuna in spring water, drained
Salt and pepper to taste

Preheat oven to 375 degrees. Spray a 9 x 13-inch baking dish with cooking spray. In a large bowl combine all ingredients; stir until well-blended. Pour the contents of the bowl into the baking dish and sprinkle the top with remaining cheese. Bake for 40 to 45 minutes, or until top is browned and casserole is bubbling. Makes 8 servings.

LEFTOVERS Á LA LOUIS

Any leftover meat—beef, ham, pork, lamb, chicken, turkey— can be put to use in this tasty casserole. The recipe was developed by Louis Lauth of Shawnee Mission, Kansas.

2 cups any leftover cooked meat, diced
1 1/2 cups cooked and chopped spaghetti
1 (4-ounce) jar sliced or diced pimientos, with juice
1/4 cup diced red bell pepper
1/2 cup diced red onion
1 (10-ounce) can cream of celery soup
1 (8-ounce) package shredded sharp cheddar cheese

Mix all ingredients in a 9 x 9-inch baking dish. Cover with foil and bake at 325 degrees for one hour.

Soups & Stews

Savory soups and stews simmer away while busy citizens mow, rake, shovel, shop or watch TV. These one-pot meals can be traditional or innovative, hearty or delicate, warm or cold, can feed a few or a crowd. Some are so simple they assemble in minutes. Others take a little longer but are well worth the effort. So sit down with a warm bowl of something delicious and enjoy a spoonful of comfort, Kansas City style.

Brie Soup

Susan's Mushroom Soup with Vermouth

Leek and Potato Soup

Baked Potato Soup

Renaissance Festival Lentil Soup with Sausage

Southwestern Mixed Bean Soup with Tortillas

White Bean Soup with
Roasted Red Pepper and Arugula

Heartland Corn Chowder

Super "Ox" Bowl Soup

Jane's Best Chicken Noodle Stew

Italian Sausage and Zucchini Soup

Burgoo

Navajo Beef Stew

Hearty Pork & Brew Stew

Persian Chili

Chunky Chicken Chili

Male Chauvinist Chili

...and more!

BRIE SOUP

1/4 cup margarine
1/2 cup chopped onion
1/2 cup thinly sliced celery
1/4 cup flour
1 1/2 cups milk
2 (15 1/2-ounce) cans chicken broth
12 ounces brie, cubed
1 apple, peeled and finely chopped

In a saucepan sauté onion and celery in margarine until tender. Blend in the flour, stirring until a smooth paste is formed. Add milk and broth. Bring to a boil over medium heat, stirring often. Boil for one minute; add brie and stir until melted. Pour into blender or food processor and process until smooth. Refrigerate several hours. Return the soup to the pan; stir in the apple and cook over medium low heat until heated through and the apple pieces are slightly softened, about 20 minutes. Makes 4 to 6 servings.

KEPT *ip: This soup can be made in advance. The longer the soup has to enhance its flavors, the better it tastes. If the brie has a very thick skin or old "aromatic" skin, you may want to remove it before cubing and melting in the soup.*

"Byerly's is a wonderful grocery store in Minneapolis and this recipe is one I adapted from their newsletter. It's a custom in my home to have a special soup before Thanksgiving and Christmas dinner. This recipe was a hands-down winner over all my other soups." Andrea Smith Kansas City, Missouri

SUSAN'S MUSHROOM SOUP WITH VERMOUTH

1 pound mushrooms
6 tablespoons butter
2 cups finely chopped onions
1/2 teaspoon sugar
1/4 cup flour
1 cup water
1 3/4 cups chicken broth
1 cup dry vermouth
1 tablespoon salt
1/4 teaspoon pepper

Slice one-third of the mushrooms and finely chop the rest. In large saucepan sauté onions and sugar in butter over medium heat, stirring frequently, for about 15 minutes or until golden. Add sliced and chopped mushrooms and sauté for 5 minutes. Stir in flour until smooth; cook for 2 minutes, stirring constantly. Pour in water and stir until smooth. Add broth, vermouth, salt and pepper and heat to boiling, stirring constantly. Reduce heat and simmer uncovered, 10 minutes. (Note: Recipe may be prepared in advance. Cover and refrigerate. To serve, heat to boiling, cover and simmer for 10 minutes.) Makes 4 to 6 servings.

CURRIED PUMPKIN BISQUE

1/4 cup (1/2 stick) butter
1 medium onion, coarsely chopped
1 clove garlic, finely chopped
1 (16-ounce) can pumpkin
4 teaspoons curry powder
1/4 teaspoon salt
1/4 teaspoon pepper
1 bay leaf
1/8 teaspoon sugar
1/8 teaspoon ground nutmeg
4 cups chicken stock
2 cups milk
1/2 cup toasted coconut, for garnish

In large saucepan cook onion and garlic in butter over medium-low heat until very soft, about 5 minutes. Stir in pumpkin, curry powder, salt, pepper, bay leaf, sugar and nutmeg. Blend in stock. Bring to boil, reduce heat to low and simmer 30 minutes. Discard bay leaf. (Note: If making in advance, prepare to this point and refrigerate until ready to reheat.) Stir in milk, and heat through. Do not boil. Garnish with toasted coconut and serve. Makes 6 to 8 first-course servings.

Sarah Huntman Reed, Kansas City, Missouri, known for her good food and generous hospitality, serves this at all Christmas holiday dinners.

SPLIT PEA SOUP

Lois Riemath of Raytown, Missouri, varies this basic soup by adding chopped ham, browned bacon pieces, or cooked and sliced sausage. She likes to garnish with shredded cheddar cheese or a few pieces of popcorn.

1 cup dry green split peas
1 medium onion, chopped
1 medium carrot, sliced
4 cups chicken broth
Salt and pepper to taste

In saucepan combine peas, onion, carrot and chicken broth. Bring to a boil, reduce heat, cover and simmer for 50 minutes or until peas are very soft. Process in small batches in blender or food processor until smooth. Makes 4 servings.

CURRIED BROCCOLI SOUP

This tasty soup can be served warm or cold. Leigh Peterman of Kansas City, Missouri, suggests substituting cauliflower for the broccoli—or using half cauliflower and half broccoli.

1 tablespoon butter
1 cup chopped onion
1 teaspoon curry powder
1/4 teaspoon salt
6 cups chopped broccoli (fresh or frozen)
2 1/2 cups no-salt added chicken broth
1 cup buttermilk

In a large saucepan sauté onions in butter until tender. Stir in curry powder and salt and cook for 1 minute. Add broccoli and chicken broth. Bring to a boil, reduce heat and simmer for 20 minutes. Purée in blender and return to saucepan. Stir in buttermilk and cook on low until heated through. Stir in additional buttermilk if necessary to thin. Makes 6 to 8 servings.

CREAMY ZUCCHINI LEEK SOUP

1 pound fresh zucchini, sliced
1/4 cup butter
1 envelope leek soup mix
2 cups milk, divided
2 cups buttermilk
Garlic salt and pepper to taste
Fresh snipped parsley, for garnish

In a saucepan sauté zucchini in butter until tender. Pour into blender jar, add soup mix and 1 cup milk; blend until smooth. Return to saucepan and add remaining milk and buttermilk. Stir to blend. Cook over low heat for 10 to 15 minutes. Do not let it boil. Season to taste with garlic salt and pepper. Serve hot, garnished with snipped parsley. Makes 4 to 6 servings.

"Because we grow zucchini, I make this soup often. At the end of summer, I shred and freeze the zucchini in individual containers so at our house 'zucchini soup's on' year round!"
Penny Seavertson
DeSoto, Kansas

LEEK AND POTATO SOUP (AKA "PUB SOUP")

2 tablespoons butter or margarine
5 slices peppered bacon, chopped
2 leeks, washed and sliced
2 (15 1/2-ounce) cans chicken broth
6 medium potatoes, peeled and quartered
1 cup cream or half and half or milk

In a large, deep saucepan sauté bacon and leeks in butter until leeks are soft. Add chicken broth and potatoes. Bring to boil, reduce heat, cover and simmer for 30 minutes or until potatoes are soft. Pour into food processor, a few cups at a time, and process until smooth. Return soup to pan, add cream and heat but do not boil. Makes 6 servings.

"This is a soup I put together after a trip to Britain. I fell in love with the British pubs and the wonderful, inexpensive meals. So I created my own version of a favorite pub soup."
Lesley Wallingford,
Fairway, Kansas

BAKED POTATO SOUP

4 large baking potatoes, baked and cooled
2/3 cup butter or margarine
2/3 cup all-purpose flour
6 cups milk
3/4 teaspoon salt
1/2 teaspoon pepper
4 green onions, chopped, divided
12 slices bacon, cooked until crisp, crumbled, divided
1 1/4 cups shredded cheddar cheese, divided
1 (8-ounce) carton sour cream

Cut potatoes in half lengthwise and scoop out pulp. Melt butter in a heavy saucepan over low heat; add flour, stirring until smooth. Cook 1 minute, stirring constantly. Gradually add milk; cook over medium heat, stirring constantly, until mixture is thickened and bubbly. Add potato pulp, salt, pepper, 2 tablespoons green onion, 1/2 cup bacon and 1 cup cheese. Cook until thoroughly heated; stir in sour cream. Add extra milk, if needed, for desired thickness. Serve garnished with remaining onion, bacon and cheese. Makes 8 to 10 servings.

SHRIMP GAZPACHO

2 cloves garlic
5 (8-ounce) packages frozen baby shrimp
6 tablespoons lemon juice
1 onion, chopped
3 cups chopped tomatoes
1 cup chopped green bell pepper
1 cup chopped cucumber
1/4 cup minced parsley
2 tablespoons minced fresh chives
2 cups tomato juice
2 teaspoons salt
4 drops Tabasco sauce
1/4 cup olive oil
Black pepper and fresh basil to taste

Rub a large bowl with the garlic cloves. Wash the shrimp and place them in the bowl; sprinkle with lemon juice. Put the onion, tomatoes, green pepper, cucumber, parsley, and chives in the bowl of a food processor and pulse to coarsely purée. Add all remaining ingredients; pulse again to blend. Pour the vegetable mixture over the shrimp. Cover and refrigerate for 2 to 24 hours before serving. Makes 8 servings.

KEPTip: *For a tangy, fresh taste, try substituting fresh chopped cilantro for the parsley in any cold soup recipe.*

Bill and Sharon Orr of Kansas City, Missouri love to entertain with summer picnics in their garden. Although Sharon admits to sometimes using her guests as "guinea pigs" and trying out new recipes on them, her Shrimp Gazpacho is a time-honored favorite that she loves to make for a crowd. She serves it in soup bowls, parfait glasses or mugs.

JAMBALAYA

1 pound smoked sausage, sliced
1 pound shrimp
1 to 2 tablespoons salt
1 to 2 tablespoons crab boil seasoning
2 (14-ounce) cans stewed tomatoes
1 to 2 cups chicken broth
3 tablespoons margarine
1 medium onion, chopped
1 green bell pepper, chopped
2 stalks celery, sliced
1 1/3 cups uncooked long grain white rice
Cajun seasoning to taste
Garlic powder to taste

Brown sausage in skillet; drain. In a large saucepan boil shrimp in crab boil and salt according to package directions. Leave the shrimp in the water used to boil them for 30 minutes to one hour after they are cooked to absorb more flavor. Rinse, cool and peel shrimp. Place the tomatoes in a blender or food processor; process until mostly liquid, although some smaller pieces of tomato should remain. Add enough chicken broth to make 4 cups of liquid; set aside. In a 5-quart saucepan sauté the onion, bell pepper and celery in margarine until onion is almost clear. Add the rice and sauté for 5 more minutes. Add sausage, shrimp and tomato/chicken broth mixture to the rice and vegetables. Season to taste with the Cajun seasoning and garlic powder. It's best to under-season at this point; you can add more later. Stir well and cover. Bring to a boil, reduce heat and simmer for 20 to 30 minutes; stirring occasionally. The jambalaya is done when the rice is tender and the liquid is almost evaporated. Makes 6 to 8 servings.

KCPT*ip: You can make this dish with chicken, shrimp or sausage or any combination of the three. It is important to watch the rice to liquid ratio.*

RENAISSANCE FESTIVAL LENTIL SOUP WITH SAUSAGE

4 cups dried lentils, washed
2 (14 1/2-ounce) cans diced tomatoes
2 large onions, chopped
16 cups beef stock
3 ribs celery, chopped
3 to 4 carrots, sliced
3 to 4 medium potatoes, cut in 1-inch pieces
1 teaspoon dried sweet basil
1 teaspoon dried thyme
1 to 2 bay leaves
1 pound smoked sausage, sliced
1/2 teaspoon liquid smoke (optional)
White pepper and salt to taste

In a large saucepan combine lentils, tomatoes, onions, beef stock, celery, carrots, potatoes, basil, thyme and bay leaves. Cook over medium heat until lentils are soft, about 1 hour or longer. In blender purée about 8 cups or two blender jars full of this mixture and add it back to the pot. Add sausage, smoke sauce, white pepper and salt and cook gently for another 10 to 15 minutes to blend the flavors. Makes 16 servings.

KCPT *ip: If you have the time to let this soup simmer for several hours, it improves both the flavor and the texture! For a vegetarian version, use a vegetable broth base instead of beef broth, and, of course, omit the sausage! (In this case, you may want to increase the amount of vegetables slightly.)*

"This soup is the all-time favorite from Mother Pockets' Soup Kitchen at the Kansas City Renaissance Festival. We begin cooking it early in the morning, in large cast iron pots over an open fire, stirring frequently with a long wooden spoon. It simmers until mid-afternoon and becomes very thick. We serve about 250 participants each day. So far the only complaints we've had are from those who have to scrub the pots!"
Pam Owens
aka Mother Pockets
Kansas City,
Missouri

SOUTHWESTERN MIXED BEAN SOUP WITH TORTILLAS

Kristin Hatch developed this fast and tasty recipe while she was working as a chef in the Southwest. Kristin, now the pastry chef at Espressly Annadores in Kansas City, Missouri, likes to offer bowls of garnish with the soup and let her guests choose their own toppings. She suggests shredded cheddar cheese, fresh minced cilantro, sour cream, and avocado.

Spicy Mix
2 teaspoons taco seasoning
1 teaspoon ground cumin
1 teaspoon dried oregano
1 teaspoon garlic powder
1/2 teaspoon dried cilantro

2 tablespoons canola oil
1/2 cup diced onions
3 teaspoons (or more, to taste) Spicy Mix
4 cups chicken broth
1 (28-ounce) can diced tomatoes
1 (15-ounce) can black beans, drained and rinsed
1 (15-ounce) can chili beans
1 (15-ounce) can corn, drained
1 (15-ounce) can hominy, drained
1 tablespoon diced green chilies
5 (6-inch) corn tortillas, cut in half, then into 1/2-inch strips

For spicy mix, combine all ingredients. Store in airtight container. For the soup, in a stockpot sauté the onions in oil over medium heat until onion is transparent. Add spicy mix and cook another 1 to 2 minutes, stirring constantly. Add chicken broth and tomatoes; turn heat to high. Add the black beans, chili beans, corn, hominy, and chilies. Stir to combine. Bring mixture to boil, then reduce heat to low. Add tortilla strips and simmer for 10 to 15 minutes. Makes 6 to 8 servings.

BLACK BEAN SOUP

1 pound dry black beans
1/2 pound bacon, chopped
3 cups chicken stock
2 tablespoons canola oil
3 stalks celery, chopped
4 carrots, chopped
3 onions, chopped
3 cloves garlic, chopped
1 (4-ounce) can mild jalapenos
1 teaspoon ground cumin
Salt to taste
1 pound spicy sausage links
1 cup dry white wine
2 tablespoons fresh lime juice

Lucylle Perry, Kansas City, Kansas, suggests garnishing the soup with a dollop of sour cream, a sprinkle of parsley and a thin slice of lime.

Rinse beans. Place in a large saucepan and cover with cold water. Bring to a boil, cover and boil for 2 minutes. Remove cover and allow beans to sit in the liquid for one hour. Drain. Combine beans, bacon, chicken stock, and enough water to cover generously. Cover and bring to a boil. Reduce heat and simmer for 2 hours or until beans are tender. In large pan sauté celery, carrots, onions, garlic, peppers and cumin in canola oil until onions are tender. Add vegetables to the pot of beans as soon as they are ready (vegetables will cook along with beans); add more water if necessary. Season with salt if desired. Just before beans are ready, cook sausage and slice into 1/2-inch pieces. Drain the bean mixture and reserve cooking liquid. Place beans and vegetables in a blender or food processor and purée, using some of the reserved liquid to make a thick soup. Return to cooking pot; stir in wine and lime juice. Add more liquid if necessary and reheat to serve. To serve, divide sausage pieces among bowls and add soup. Makes 8 to 10 servings.

SPICY COUNTRY BEAN SOUP

Lee Major,
Shawnee Mission,
Kansas, first made
this flavorful soup
during a rainy
weekend in the
Ozarks. Several
experimental
versions brought
him to the recipe
which has become
a family favorite.
Lee suggests
putting together
your own custom
bean mix. Go to a
health food store
and get a scoop
of any beans that
strike your fancy.
Don't forget to
include lentils
and split peas.

2 cups mixed dry beans, washed
1 tablespoon salt
2 quarts water
2 ham hocks
1 clove garlic, pressed
1 (16-ounce) can tomatoes, with juice
1 large onion, diced
3 carrots, sliced
3 stalks celery, with leaves, sliced
1 green bell pepper, chopped
3 tablespoons fresh lemon juice
1 bay leaf
1 tablespoon chili powder
2 tablespoons black pepper
1 tablespoon basil
1 teaspoon each: parsley, summer savory, cumin seeds,
  thyme, sage, oregano, rosemary, marjoram

Place beans in a large pan with enough water to cover and a tablespoon of salt. Soak overnight. In the morning, discard water, rinse beans and put in a large soup pot with all ingredients. Bring to a boil; reduce to simmer. After two hours, remove ham hocks, remove meat from bone, discard bone, rind and fat. Return meat to pot. Cook all day (at least 8 to 10 hours). Remove bay leaf before serving. Makes 10 to 12 servings.

BONNIE'S WHITE BEAN SOUP WITH ROASTED RED PEPPER AND ARUGULA

2 tablespoons olive oil
1 small onion, peeled and diced
2 (15 1/2-ounce) cans white northern beans, drained
1 (7 1/4-ounce) jar roasted red peppers, drained and chopped
2 (10-ounce) cans chicken broth
1/2 cup fresh chopped arugula or basil, for garnish

In a saucepan sauté the onion in olive oil until transparent, about 5 minutes. Add the beans, red peppers, and chicken broth. Bring to a boil; reduce heat and simmer for 10 minutes. Serve each bowl garnished with the chopped arugula or basil. Makes 4 servings.

Food guru Bonnie Winston, Kansas City, Missouri, whips up this soup when she's hungry yet pressed for time. The flavors are sunny and bold, while the preparation is easy.

HEARTLAND CORN CHOWDER

1/2 pound apple-smoked bacon, diced
1 onion, peeled and chopped
1 red bell pepper, seeded and chopped
1 green bell pepper, seeded and chopped
6 cups fresh corn, divided
1 cup chopped smoked chicken or ham
4 potatoes, peeled and chopped
3 cups half and half, divided
1/4 teaspoon ground red pepper
Salt and pepper to taste

In a large saucepan sauté the bacon, onion, and peppers until the vegetables are crisp-tender. Add 4 cups of the corn, the smoked chicken, and the potatoes. Add just enough water to cover. Bring to a boil; reduce heat and simmer, covered, for 1 hour. In a food processor, purée the remaining 2 cups of corn with 2 cups half and half; add the mixture to the soup. Simmer for 30 minutes. Just before serving, add the rest of the half and half, the ground red pepper and season to taste. Makes 6 servings.

Keitha Kaminsky, Kansas City, Missouri, created this recipe for a lovely colorful chowder which tastes great either warm or cold. Fresh corn is best, but if it's not available, try frozen or canned.

MAQUE CHOUX

3 tablespoons bacon drippings
2 medium yellow onions, chopped
2 cloves garlic, minced
1 medium red or yellow bell pepper, chopped
3 (14-ounce) cans chopped tomatoes or 5 fresh tomatoes
2 tablespoons sugar
12 to 14 ears fresh corn, kernels cut from cobs
2 tablespoons cayenne pepper
1 (14-ounce) can condensed milk
Salt and pepper to taste
3 pounds medium shrimp, peeled and deveined

In large stock pot, cook onions, garlic, and pepper in bacon drippings until onions are clear. Add tomatoes, sugar, corn, cayenne pepper, milk and enough water to cover. Bring soup to a light boil and add salt and pepper to taste. Reduce heat and simmer for at least 30 minutes until corn is tender. Add shrimp and cook for another 10 to 15 minutes. Makes 15 servings.

KEPT *ip: Use a butcher knife to cut corn off cob; use the back side of blade to scrape "milk" from cob. You can use frozen or canned corn, but the flavor doesn't compare.*

"I'm from southern Louisiana and remember having this often while growing up. This recipe is one I developed from the one I learned from my family. I've fixed it many times for friends. Serve with crackers or over rice."
Tina Fontenot
Raytown, Missouri

SUPER "OX" BOWL SOUP

4 pounds oxtails
1 large onion, coarsely chopped
1 (1-ounce) package onion soup mix
1 tablespoon tapioca or flour
2 (14-ounce) cans chopped tomatoes
1 (12-ounce) can whole kernel corn, drained
1 (15-ounce) can green beans, drained
1 (15-ounce) can lima beans, drained
1/4 teaspoon ground red pepper
2 teaspoons strong ground coffee
1 teaspoon chili powder
1 teaspoon oregano
2 drops liquid smoke
2 capfuls white vinegar
2 ounces dry vermouth
3 carrots, sliced
2 stalks celery, chopped
3 cloves garlic, chopped
Salt to taste
1/2 pound diced country ham (optional, but very good)

In a large pot combine oxtails, onion and soup mix . Cover with 4 inches of water and simmer for 4 hours. Cover and refrigerate overnight. Skim fat off top. With slotted spoon, remove oxtails and separate meat from bone. Over medium heat, stir tapioca into broth; continue to stir until thickened. Return meat to pot. Add all remaining ingredients, reduce heat and simmer for at least 2 hours. Makes 12 servings.

KCPT *ip: Can substitute 2 large potatoes, cut into large chunks or 1/2 pound cooked pasta for lima beans. Add during the last hour. Because potatoes will absorb some of the seasoning, amounts may need to be adjusted.*

Bill Hickok, Shawnee Mission, Kansas, makes this hearty soup often during the winter and it's always on the menu for his traditional Super Bowl Party. He recommends serving with cornbread.

EASY CHICKEN SOUP

"This is a very 'forgiving' soup— you really can't go wrong with it! Substitute potatoes, black beans or noodles for the rice. For a spicier version, replace the stewed tomatoes with a can of tomatoes and green chilies."
Dee Barwick
Fairway, Kansas

1 tablespoon butter
4 chicken breast halves, with bones and skin
3 large yellow onions, chopped
2 stalks celery, including leaves, sliced
2 carrots, sliced
1 bay leaf
4 cups chicken broth
2 cups cooked brown rice (slightly undercooked)
1 (16-ounce) package frozen mixed vegetables
1 (15-ounce) can stewed tomatoes
1 tablespoon fresh lemon juice
1/2 cup dry vermouth (optional)

In large sauce pan cook breasts in butter over medium heat until light brown, about 10 minutes. Stir in onions, celery, carrots and bay leaf; cook on low until onions are very soft, about one hour. Add broth, rice and vegetables. Cover; cook on low for 60 to 90 minutes. Remove meat from bone, chop and return to pot. Add tomatoes, lemon juice and vermouth if using. Cook for another 30 minutes. Makes 6 servings.

RUSSIAN MENNONITE CHICKEN NOODLE SOUP

"The secret to this unusal soup is the star anise. I got the recipe while researching an article in Western Kansas."
Judith Fertig
Overland Park, Kansas

10 cups chicken stock
4 whole star anise
10 whole black peppercorns
6 bay leaves
1/3 cup chopped fresh parsley
2 to 3 cups fresh thin-cut noodles (or one 12-ounce bag)
Salt and pepper to taste

Put stock in large soup pot. Combine star anise, peppercorns and bay leaves in a cheesecloth bag; put in stock, bring to a boil, then reduce heat and simmer for 30 minutes. Remove bag; add parsley and noodles. Let sit for 20 minutes. Makes 8 servings.

JANE'S BEST CHICKEN NOODLE STEW

3 tablespoons olive oil
2 yellow onions, chopped
5 ribs celery, sliced
3 to 5 cloves garlic, finely minced
1 1/2 cups hot water
Kosher salt to taste
2 pounds boneless, skinless chicken breasts, cut in
   1-inch pieces
5 carrots, sliced
3/4 cup minced parsley, divided
10 cups chicken stock
1 1/2 cups sliced fresh mushrooms
1 (10-ounce) package frozen thick egg noodles
1/2 bunch cilantro, minced, for garnish

In soup pot sauté yellow onion and celery in olive oil over medium-high heat for 3 to 4 minutes. Add garlic, stir and continue to sauté for 2 minutes. Add hot water and salt and stir. Layer chicken, carrots and half of the parsley atop the sautéed mixture; do not stir. When water begins to steam, immediately reduce heat to low; cover pot with tight-fitting lid and simmer for 30 minutes. Add chicken stock and mushrooms, stir and raise heat to medium high. When liquid comes to a boil add frozen egg noodles; stir gently to separate noodles; reduce heat and simmer, uncovered, for 25 to 30 minutes, stirring occasionally, until noodles are desired tenderness. Add remaining parsley and allow to wilt in stew before serving. Garnish with minced cilantro. Makes 6 servings.

"The secret to the rich full flavor of this stew is in the process of steaming the chicken, parsley and carrots in layers atop the onion, celery and garlic before adding the chicken stock. Cilantro (1/2 bunch, minced) may be substituted for parsley. Canned sliced mushrooms may be used in place of fresh mushrooms."
Jane Berkowitz
Kansas City,
Missouri

ITALIAN SAUSAGE AND ZUCCHINI SOUP

"I never get tired of this soup. For me it falls into the 'comfort food' category. I've prepared it for tailgate parties and super bowl parties. And it's a great way to use up that end-of-season zucchini because it freezes so well. Serve with warm Italian bread and a nice red wine."
Linda Hill
Raytown, Missouri

1 1/2 pounds Italian sausage, casings removed
2 cups celery, cut in 1/2-inch pieces
2 pounds zucchini, cut in 1/2-inch pieces
1 cup chopped onion
2 (28-ounce) cans whole tomatoes
1 teaspoon salt
1 teaspoon Italian seasoning
1 teaspoon oregano
1 teaspoon sugar
1/2 teaspoon basil
1/4 teaspoon garlic powder
2 green bell peppers, cut in 1/2-inch pieces
Freshly grated parmesan cheese, for garnish

In a stock pot brown sausage; drain. Return meat to pot and add celery, zucchini, onion, tomatoes, salt, Italian seasoning, oregano, sugar, basil and garlic powder. Cook on high until it just comes to a boil, reduce heat and simmer until vegetables are tender, approximately one hour. Add green pepper and heat through. Serve with parmesan cheese sprinkled on top. Makes 6 servings.

BURGOO STEW

2 pounds boneless, skinless chicken breasts, cubed
2 pounds boneless lean beef, cubed
4 quarts water
2 green bell peppers, chopped
1 red bell pepper, chopped
2 (16-ounce) cans peeled tomatoes, with juice
2 cups diced raw potatoes
2 cups diced onions
2 cups chopped okra
1 (16-ounce) can corn, with liquid
1 (16-ounce) can butter beans, drained
3 large carrots, diced
3 large ribs celery, diced
4 cloves garlic, mashed
6 bay leaves
1 1/2 cups dry sherry
Salt and pepper to taste

Place chicken and beef in a large soup pot with water. Simmer for about 2 hours or until meat is tender. Add peppers, tomatoes, potatoes, onions, okra, corn, beans, carrots, celery, garlic, and bay leaves. Cover and cook over low heat 6 to 8 hours or until the mixture is very thick. Add sherry one hour before serving. Add salt and pepper to taste. Makes 24 one-cup servings.

Mary Loberg, Shawnee Mission, Kansas, thinks that a party on the first Saturday in May is the perfect way to give an early welcome to summer. Over a period of ten years her Kentucky Derby gathering grew from ten people to sixty, thanks mostly to this Burgoo Stew and the Cheese & Garlic Grits (page 43) that kept people coming back for more!

NAVAJO BEEF STEW

"This is a moderni-zation of an old Navajo recipe that was made with mutton and cooked over an open fire."
Claire Northamer
Kansas City,
Kansas

2 tablespoons cooking oil
1 pound boneless stew beef, cut in 1-inch cubes
1 large yellow onion, chopped
2 cloves garlic, diced
4 cups beef broth
2 bay leaves
1 cup whole kernel corn
2 (4 1/2-ounce) cans chopped green chilies
1 jalapeno pepper, chopped (optional)
3 medium potatoes, diced
2 tablespoons ground cumin
1/2 teaspoon salt
1/2 teaspoon pepper

In large heavy pot cook beef in oil until almost brown. Add onion and garlic and finish browning. Add broth and bay leaves. Bring to boil; reduce heat and simmer for 1 hour. Remove bay leaves. Add corn, chilies, jalapeno pepper, potatoes, cumin, salt and pepper. Bring to boil; reduce heat and simmer 45 minutes, stirring occasionally. Add more broth or water if soup seems too dry. Makes 6 servings.

GREEN CHILI STEW

1 pound pork, cubed
1 Anaheim pepper, roasted and chopped
1 (16-ounce) can tomatoes and diced green chilies
1 cup chicken broth
2 tablespoons chili powder
1 pound potatoes (about 3 medium), peeled and cubed
1 jalapeno pepper, chopped
1 teaspoon vinegar
1 teaspoon salt
2 tablespoons jalapeno pepper sauce

In a large skillet sear cubed pork until brown. In a large pan combine pork, Anaheim pepper, tomatoes, broth and chili powder. Bring to a boil; reduce heat, cover and simmer for one hour. Add potatoes, jalapeno pepper, vinegar, salt and pepper sauce. Cover and continue to simmer for approximately 1 hour or until potatoes are tender. Makes 4 to 6 servings.

KCPT *ip: This stew goes great with warmed flour tortillas sprinkled with shredded cheddar cheese and Jicama and Red Sweet Pepper Salad (page XX).*

"My father, Herb Long, of Peculiar, Missouri, had never cooked much, but one day after he retired he saw this recipe demonstrated on a CIA Cooking show on KCPT. Thus began his yearly Christmas-time dinner for our family. My mother still does the cooking for everything else, but this is his specialty and Christmas isn't complete without it."
Karen Long
Peculiar, Missouri

HEARTY PORK & BREW STEW

*Frank Cooper,
Kansas City,
Missouri, has made
this stew for many
years. He often
garnishes with
green peas. To
round out the
menu, Frank
suggests warm
homemade bread
and fresh fruit or
salad. For dessert?
Something rich and
creamy. Perhaps
Coconut Rum Flan
with Starfruit
(page 172).*

3 pounds boneless pork shoulder, in 1 1/2-inch cubes
2 tablespoon oil
2 teaspoons salt
1/2 teaspoon freshly ground black pepper
1 teaspoon ground rosemary
3 tablespoons flour
1 pint dark beer
1 1/2 cups beef broth
4 medium carrots, sliced in 1/4-inch slices
4 medium potatoes, sliced in 1/2-inch slices
4 stalks celery, sliced in 1/2-inch slices
4 medium onions, quartered

Preheat oven to 300 degrees. Trim fat from pork and pat dry. In a large skillet, brown meat in oil a few pieces at a time; place in flameproof casserole. Add salt, pepper, and rosemary to meat and cook over low heat. Stir in flour until it disappears. Add beer and beef broth. Bring to a simmer, cover and place in oven. Bake for 45 minutes; skim fat. Add carrots, potatoes, celery and onions; cover and return to oven for 1 hour or until vegetables and meat are tender. Makes 8 to 10 servings.

PERSIAN CHILI STEW

2 tablespoons cooking oil
1 small white onion, diced
1 clove garlic, minced
4 small carrots, diced
2 medium potatoes, diced
2 celery stalks from center, diced
1/4 green bell pepper, diced
1 1/2 pounds lean ground chuck
1 teaspoon chopped cilantro
1 bay leaf
1 teaspoon chili powder
1/4 teaspoon coriander
1/4 teaspoon cumin
1 (15-ounce) can tomatoes
1 (8-ounce) can tomato sauce
Salt and pepper to taste
1 (15-ounce) can red kidney beans
Shredded cheese and/or sour cream, for garnish

In a medium pan sauté onion and garlic in cooking oil. Add carrots, potatoes, celery, and green pepper. Cook over low heat for about 15 minutes, until vegetable are slightly tender. Meanwhile, in large skillet sauté ground chuck; add vegetables to meat. add cilantro, bay leaf, chili powder, coriander, cumin, tomatoes and tomato sauce; stir well. Cover and cook over medium heat for 15 minutes. Add salt and pepper to taste. Add kidney beans. Cook for 10 minutes. Makes 6 to 8 servings.

"This recipe is a combination of traditional chili and Persian stew which I developed because, for me, most chilies have too much meat and beans. The potatoes and beans absorb the seasonings, giving a wonderful hearty flavor. I like to serve with toasted pita bread."
Shirin Khodayari
Overland Park, Kansas

CHUNKY CHICKEN CHILI

Vegetable cooking spray
1 1/2 cups chopped onion
1 cup chopped green bell pepper
3 jalapeno peppers, chopped (or 4-ounce can diced chilies)
3 cloves garlic, minced
2 tablespoons chili powder
2 teaspoons ground cumin
1/2 teaspoon dried whole oregano
4 cups bite-size pieces cooked chicken breast (about 2 pounds skinless, boneless chicken breasts)
1 cup water
1/2 teaspoon ground red pepper
1/4 teaspoon black pepper
1 tablespoon worcestershire sauce
1 tablespoon Dijon mustard
1 (14 1/2-ounce) can stewed tomatoes
1 (14 1/2-ounce) can chicken broth
1 (12-ounce) bottle chili sauce
1 (16-ounce) can great northern beans, drained
1 1/4 cups peeled, diced avocado, for garnish
1 1/4 cups chopped purple onion, for garnish
1/2 cup sour cream, for garnish

Coat a dutch oven with cooking spray; place over medium heat until hot. Add onion, green pepper, jalapeno peppers, and garlic; sauté 5 minutes. Add chili powder, cumin and oregano; cook 2 minutes. Add chicken, water, red pepper, black pepper, worcestershire sauce, mustard, tomatoes, broth, and chili sauce. Bring to a boil; cover, reduce heat and simmer 20 minutes. Add beans and cook another 5 minutes. Top with avocado, onion and sour cream. Makes 8 to 10 servings.

KCPTip: *Start off with 1 tablespoon chili powder and add to taste. This dish can get overly spicy.*

CASHEW CHICKEN CHILI

2 roasted red bell peppers (skin, seeds and veins removed)

1 small can chopped jalapenos, drained (hot or mild)

1 1/2 cups roasted cashews (whole, halves or pieces), divided

2 1/2 cups chicken stock, divided

3 tablespoons olive oil

2 medium onions, chopped

4 cloves garlic, minced

1 teaspoon salt

1 1/2 teaspoons ground cumin

2 teaspoons chili powder

2 whole chicken breasts, skin removed, washed and dried

1/2 cup chopped fresh cilantro, divided

1 (15-ounce) can diced tomatoes, with juice

2 ounces bittersweet or semi-sweet chocolate

1 (14 1/2-ounce) can kidney beans, rinsed and drained

Jane Berkowitz, Kansas City, Missouri, is famous in her Westport neighborhood for cooking delectable soups. She developed this recipe through much trial and error. The results are unique and delicious!

In blender combine roasted red peppers, jalapenos, 1/2 cup of the cashews and 1 cup chicken stock. Purée while slowly adding remaining 1 1/2 cups of chicken stock until smooth. In soup pot sauté onion and garlic in hot oil over medium heat until onions are tender. Add salt, cumin and chili powder, stir well and continue to sauté for 1 minute. Add chicken breasts, turning to thoroughly coat with sautéed mixture. Stir in red pepper purée, 1/4 cup chopped cilantro, and tomatoes with juice. Cover and simmer for 45 minutes, stirring occasionally, until chicken is tender and thoroughly cooked. Remove chicken breasts, allow to cool slightly, and using two forks, shred chicken into bite-sized pieces. Discard bones and return meat to soup pot. Stir in chocolate and beans. Cook over moderate heat, stirring frequently, until heated through and chocolate is melted. (Note: Can be made to this point up to two days in advance. Reheat before adding remaining ingredients.) Add remaining 1/4 cup chopped cilantro and 1 cup cashews. Stir to combine and serve immediately. Makes 4 to 6 servings.

MALE CHAUVINIST CHILI

Though the name may date it, this hearty, spicy chili has never gone out of style with Bill Hunt's friends. Bill, a resident of Prairie Village, Kansas, adapted this recipe from one he found in a magazine several years ago. He suggests making it the day before you plan to serve.

6 slices bacon, chopped
1 pound hamburger
1 pound hot Italian bulk sausage
1 large onion, chopped
2 cloves garlic, minced
1 jalapeno pepper, chopped
1 green bell pepper, chopped
1 cup dry red wine
1/2 cup worcestershire sauce
1 teaspoon dry mustard
1 teaspoon celery seed
1 1/2 teaspoons chili powder
1/2 teaspoon salt
1 1/2 teaspoons black pepper
6 cups coarsely chopped Italian tomatoes
1 (15-ounce) can pinto beans
1 (15-ounce) can kidney beans
1 (15-ounce) can garbanzo beans

In large pan brown bacon, hamburger and sausage; drain and set aside. In same pan sauté onion, garlic, jalapeno pepper and green pepper. In large soup pot combine meat and vegetables and add all remaining ingredients. Cook, covered, over low heat for 3 to 4 hours. Makes 8 servings.

BARNETT'S "ONE OF A KIND" CHILI

**12 pounds of hamburger (don't get fancy and substitute
     ground round or steak, you need hamburger)**
2 (46-ounce) large cans of tomato juice
6 packets of Williams chili mix
Salt to taste
1 (5-ounce) bottle of Tabasco sauce
3 (4 1/2-ounce size) cans of chili powder
2 bunches of scallions
6 whole tomatoes
4 green bell peppers
2 (2-ounce) boxes of dry red peppers (the red hot kind)
6 (14 1/2-ounce) cans kidney beans
**6 (14 1/2-ounce) cans chili beans (the different colors
     look pretty)**
**Lots of hungry people and lots of cola or your favorite
     beverage**

If there were a prize for most unique recipe, it would be awarded to Barnett Helzberg, Jr., Kansas City, Missouri for this original chili. We present it here in his own words— just as he wrote it. Follow at your own risk.

Get a very large pot (industrial size) which will hold the entire batch, or the alternative is to mess up most of the pots in the house. (Your wife will love this.) Brown the meat in the pot by starting with a low heat and pouring all of the meat in, squishing it around as you go and at least one of the large cans of tomato juice and the meat will brown in the solution. Turn up heat but do not burn. Stir constantly. Later, heat should be medium to medium high. Add the six packets of Williams Chili Mix, one at a time, and crush so you don't find any lumps. Add some salt as you go, but be careful, since salt is very hard to take out once it is added in. Add 20 drops of Tabasco at this point and add a half can of chili powder.

While this brew is bubbling, clean the scallions, dice them finely and then add them to the brew. Tomatoes, cut them into eighths and add. Green peppers, cut into small pieces and add. Now the challenge begins. Be sure during all of this period to stir regularly. (Again, we stress the relationship of burning the bottom of the pot to the lowering of quality of the chili batch.) Add the rest of the tomato juice so that you have a semi-soupy mixture. Remember that much of the moisture will cook off, but you want to end up with a very thick chili.

Use blender to grind up a dozen of the red peppers. After you have cut the blender off, do not go near the blender and do not open up the top of the blender for three minutes, inasmuch as these peppers can float in the air and be quite uncomfortable to the throat and eyes. After they have settled fully into the bottom of the blender, gingerly move the blender to the chili pot and add the peppers to the chili. At this point add another half of a can of chili powder. Taste the solution, because the skill will be involved in balancing the proper amount of salt, Tabasco and hot red peppers, according to your own personal taste. Basically, you will find that the proper combination will burn upon entry into the oral cavity and also after it has been ingested into your system. The latter phenomenon is referred to as "after burn."

It is desirable to have a large appetite and friends who have large appetites, as the tasting process is perhaps the most sensitive though pleasurable part of this task. Leave grease on top of the chili. It is the medium through which the seasoning flows to the furthest extremities of the chili pot. When you dish out the chili, the grease can be drained off of each individual spoonful. Cook the chili for a good 3 hours that first day—the more, the merrier. When you have finished your day's cooking, let the pot rest, in refrigerator, overnight for the following two days. Continue to taste the batch and balance the salt, Tabasco and dry red peppers. In fact, this is a necessity inasmuch as the "fermentation process" will be contributing its own little bit to your success.

At the end of the second day, reheat the chili and invite those you love most in the world to enjoy your labor of love. One hour prior to their arrival, wash the beans in a colander and add them to the chili.

Breads

The aroma of bread baking has wafted through our town since it was known as Chez les Canses and welcomed the ethnic breads we've come to love— Jewish Challah, Irish Soda, French and Sourdough to name a few. As the town expanded, so did our tastes. Soon tea rooms welcomed white-gloved ladies in downtown department stores where a cup of tea with a slice of blueberry banana bread restored their energy. Now with the popularity of bread machines, a new generation of Kansas Citians wakes to the aroma of bread baking, and the beat goes on...

Savory Wild Rice Muffins

Runners' Muffins

Raspberry Almond Tea Muffins

Sour Cream Nutbread

Orange Cinnamon Bread with Glaze

Blueberry Banana Bread

Best Prune Bread Ever

Paddy's Pub Irish Soda Bread

Plum Delicious Biscuits

Sour Cream Cinnamon Rolls

Sunflower Club Potato Rolls

Sandy's Easy Crescent Rolls

Tuscan Bread

Challah

Italian Sourdough Bread

Greek Isle Bread

Parmesan Peppercorn Bread

Prairie Sage Cornmeal Bread

...and more!

SAVORY WILD RICE MUFFINS

3/4 cup flour
2 teaspoons sugar
1 teaspoon salt
1/4 teaspoon white pepper
1 cup cooked wild rice
1/4 cup chopped pecans, lightly toasted
3 tablespoons melted butter
1 egg
1 cup milk
3 tablespoons fresh chopped chives

Preheat oven to 450 degrees. Butter 12 muffin cups. Combine flour, sugar, salt, and pepper. Combine rice and nuts with melted butter. Beat egg with milk. Add flour mixture alternately with milk mixture to rice. Blend well, but do not beat. Fold in the chives. Spoon about 1/4 cup batter into each cup. Bake for 12 to 15 minutes. Makes 12 muffins.

KCPT *ip: Serve flavored butters to add a zip to your favorite bread. For savory butters, combine 1 stick softened butter with any of the following:*

- *1 teaspoon dried basil, crushed*
- *1/2 teaspoon each dried oregano and thyme, crushed*
- *2 tablespoons grated romano cheese and 2 teaspoons chopped chives*

For sweet butters, combine 1 stick softened butter with any of these:

- *1/2 cup finely chopped almonds and 1/4 cup apricot preserves*
- *1 tablespoon orange liqueur, 1 tablespoon powdered sugar and 1 teaspoon finely grated orange peel*

"These muffins are so easy to make! Especially if you cook an entire box of wild rice in advance and keep it handy in the freezer. Serve them with herb butter."
Joy Hesler
Shawnee Mission, Kansas

RUNNERS' MUFFINS

1 cup unbleached white flour
2 cups whole wheat flour
3 teaspoons cinnamon
4 teaspoons baking soda
1/2 teaspoon salt
3 well-ripened bananas
3/4 cup margarine
1 cup water
1 1/2 cups raisins
1/4 cup buttermilk
1 cup chopped walnuts
1 1/2 cups brown sugar
3 eggs
3 1/2 cups rolled oats
1/2 cup wheat germ
1 cup chocolate chips

Preheat oven to 350 degrees. Butter 36 muffin cups. Combine white flour, whole wheat flour, cinnamon, baking soda and salt in a large mixing bowl; set aside. Process bananas in a food processor. Add margarine and continue to blend. Combine water and raisins in a microwave-safe container and heat for 1 1/2 minutes in microwave. Add raisin-water mixture, buttermilk, and walnuts to banana mixture and process on high until well blended. Pour into a large mixing bowl and add brown sugar and eggs. Mix until just combined; do not overbeat. Add flour mixture, until just combined. Add rolled oats, wheat germ and chocolate chips. Mix until combined. Fill muffin tins 3/4 full and bake for 15 to 20 minutes. Makes 36 muffins.

KCPT*ip: Nuts will yield more flavor if they are lightly browned before adding to batter. Spread on a cookie sheet in a single layer and bake at 350 degrees for 5 to 8 minutes until very lightly browned. Watch carefully and stir once or twice to avoid burning.*

RASPBERRY ALMOND TEA MUFFINS

8 ounces whole almonds
2/3 cup plus 1/4 cup sugar
1 teaspoon almond extract, divided
2 cups all-purpose flour
2 teaspoons baking powder
1/2 teaspoon salt
1 cup milk
1/2 cup (1 stick) butter, melted and cooled
1 teaspoon vanilla extract
3/4 cup flaked coconut
6 tablespoons seedless raspberry jam

"Recipe for a perfect treat: Sit down in a favorite chair, have a cup of tea and enjoy one (or two) of these fragrant, delicious muffins."
Jane Guthrie
Kansas City, Missouri

Preheat oven to 350 degrees. Lightly grease 3 mini-muffin tins. Spread almonds on a baking sheet and lightly toast in oven for 7 to 10 minutes or until the almonds are slightly browned. Put almonds in bowl of food processor with 1/4 cup sugar; process until the mixture resembles fine crumbs. Add 1/2 teaspoon almond extract and blend again; set aside. Combine flour, 2/3 cup sugar, baking powder, and salt in a large bowl. In a separate bowl combine milk, melted butter, vanilla extract and remaining almond extract. Make a well in the center of the flour mixture; add the liquid ingredients and stir to blend. Fold in the coconut. Spoon half of the batter into the prepared tins. Place a tea-spoonful of almond filling and 1/2 teaspoon raspberry jam on top of each portion of batter to form the middle of the muffins. Spoon remaining half of the batter on top of filling. Bake 15 to 20 minutes, or until light brown. Cool in the muffin tins for 5 minutes, then turn out onto wire racks. Makes 3 dozen mini-muffins.

SOUR CREAM NUTBREAD

Doris M. Sanders, Kansas City, Missouri, makes this no-shortening bread often. She likes to use English Walnuts but suggests trying different nuts for a little variety.

1 cup brown sugar
1 egg, well beaten
1 cup sour cream
1 teaspoon soda
1 1/2 cups flour
1/4 teaspoon salt
1 cup nuts, coarsely chopped

Preheat oven to 350 degrees. Spray a 9 x 5 loaf pan with cooking spray. Combine sugar and egg, blending well. Add sour cream, mix well. Add soda, flour, salt, and mix well but do not beat. Stir in nuts. Bake for one hour or until lightly brown. Makes 1 loaf.

BEST PRUNE BREAD EVER

"If using pitted prunes use approximately 25 prunes, cut into quarters. Using prunes with pits really does make the final product taste better. Why, who knows! Serving this bread at Christmas time is one of our family's traditions. The recipe is an old one from Mary Regan."
Karen Regan
Kansas City,
Missouri

1/2 pound extra large prunes, with pits
   (approximately 18 prunes)
2 teaspoons baking soda
2 cups boiling water
1/2 cup (1 stick) butter or margarine
2 cups sugar
2 eggs
1 teaspoon vanilla
4 cups flour
1 teaspoon salt
1 cup raisins (can also use golden raisins)
1/2 cup nuts, chopped (optional)

Preheat oven to 350 degrees. Grease two 9 x 5 loaf pans. Remove pits from prunes and cut each prune into quarters. Dissolve baking soda in boiling water. Add prunes, mix and let stand until cool. Meanwhile, cream butter or margarine and sugar in large bowl. Add eggs and vanilla. In small bowl combine flour and salt; add gradually to batter, and as batter begins to thicken add water (from the soaking prunes) alternately with flour. Stir in raisins, prunes and nuts. Divide batter into pans and bake for 1 to 1 1/2 hours or until toothpick inserted in center comes out clean. Makes 2 loaves.

ORANGE CINNAMON BREAD WITH GLAZE

6 tablespoons butter
1 1/3 cups sugar, divided
2 eggs
Grated rind of 1 orange
1 teaspoon cinnamon
Pinch of salt
1 1/2 cups sifted all-purpose flour
1/2 teaspoon baking soda
1/2 teaspoon baking powder
1/2 cup plain yogurt
Juice of 1 orange

Preheat oven to 350 degrees. Grease and lightly flour a 8 1/2 x 4 1/2 loaf pan. In mixing bowl cream together butter and 1 cup of sugar. Add eggs and beat until light and fluffy. Add the orange rind, cinnamon and salt; mix well. Sift the flour with the baking soda and baking powder. Stir the flour mixture and the yogurt alternately into the butter and sugar mixture, beginning and ending with flour. Pour batter into loaf pan. Bake 1 hour and fifteen minutes or until a toothpick inserted in the center comes out clean. While the cake is baking, in a small pan dissolve the remaining sugar in the orange juice. Place the pan over low heat and stir until the sugar is completely dissolved. When the cake is done, place the loaf pan on a cooling rack. Pour the orange juice/sugar mixture over the hot cake. Let cool completely before removing from pan. Makes 1 loaf.

KEPT *ip: Add a "surprise" filling to your favorite sweet bread. Combine 6 ounces cream cheese with 1/3 cup granulated sugar, 1 large egg and 1 tablespoon grated orange (or lemon) zest. Pour two-thirds of batter in prepared pan, top with the filling, then top with remaining batter. Lightly swirl with a knife. Bake as directed until bread is lightly brown and firm to the touch.*

"During the early eighties I sold gourmet breads to Clearly Nature's Own (now the Wild Oats on Main) and The Corner Restaurant in Westport. This orange bread was on The Corner's menu for more than two years."
Lisa Waterman Gray
Overland Park, Kansas

BLUEBERRY BANANA BREAD

*Evelyn Toner,
Kansas City,
Missouri, also likes
to use this recipe
for blueberry
muffins. One half
the bread recipe
makes 1 1/2 dozen
muffins. Bake
muffins at 375
degrees for about
20 minutes.*

2 cups whole wheat flour
1 cup white flour
1 1/3 cup sugar
4 teaspoons baking powder
1/2 teaspoon salt
1 1/2 cups quick-cooking rolled oats
1/2 cup vegetable oil
4 eggs
2 cups mashed bananas (about 4 large)
2 cups blueberries (fresh or frozen)

Preheat oven to 350 degrees. Oil two 8 1/2 x 4 1/2 loaf pans. Combine flours, sugar, baking powder and salt. Stir in oats. In a blender, purée oil, eggs and bananas; stir into dry ingredients just until mixed. Stir in blueberries. Pour batter into pans and bake for approximately 60 minutes. Let bread cool in pans 10 minutes, then remove to cool completely on wire racks. Makes 2 loaves.

PADDY'S PUB IRISH SODA BREAD

*"Top of the Tower
Restaurant was a
popular spot in
Kansas City in
the sixties. It
featured several
international
cuisines and this
recipe came from
Paddy's Pub.
Everyone in my
family loves it.
Sharon Cottitta
Kansas City,
Missouri*

3 cups flour
1/3 cup sugar
1 tablespoon baking powder
1 teaspoon baking soda
1 teaspoon salt
1 egg, beaten slightly
2 cups buttermilk
1/4 cup melted butter

Preheat oven to 325 degrees. Grease a 9 x 5 loaf pan. Combine flour, sugar, baking powder, baking soda and salt in a large mixing bowl. Stir to mix well. Blend egg with buttermilk; add to flour mixture. Mix by hand just enough to blend ingredients. Stir in melted butter and mix well. Pour into pan. Bake 65 to 75 minutes. Do not underbake! Remove from pan and cool completely on wire rack. Place in airtight wrap or container and store at least 8 hours before slicing. Makes 1 loaf.

BUTTERMILK REFRIGERATOR BISCUITS

1 (1/4-ounce) package dry yeast
1/2 cup warm water
5 cups flour
3 teaspoons baking powder
1 teaspoon salt
1 teaspoon baking soda
3 tablespoons sugar
3/4 cup solid shortening
2 cups buttermilk

Dissolve yeast in warm water to proof and cover loosely; set aside. Sift together flour, baking powder, salt, soda and sugar. Cut in shortening. Add buttermilk and mix. Add water and yeast mixture; mix until moistened. Cover bowl and refrigerate until needed. When ready to use, preheat oven to 375 degrees. Take amount of dough needed (one-fourth of the dough will make 1 dozen biscuits), roll on floured board to 1/2-inch thickness and cut with biscuit cutter. Bake on cookie sheet 12 to 15 minutes. Makes 4 dozen biscuits.

Is there a better Sunday morning luxury than hot biscuits? However you choose to top them—jam, butter or sausage gravy— you'll be glad Mellody Allee of Sedalia, Missouri, shared this recipe which makes serving fresh-baked biscuits a breeze!

PLUM DELICIOUS BISCUITS

1/2 cup sugar
1/2 teaspoon cinnamon
10 unbaked biscuits, homemade or canned
1/3 cup butter, melted
10 teaspoons plum preserves

Heat oven to 350 degrees. Combine sugar and cinnamon. Dip both sides of biscuits in butter, then in sugar mixture. Place on ungreased cookie sheet. With thumb make deep indentation in center of each biscuit. Fill with 1 teaspoon preserves. Bake for 15 to 20 minutes or until golden brown.

"These biscuits are always popular whether they're served warm out of the oven or the next day. Use any kind of preserve you prefer."
Colleen Adams Kansas City, Missouri

SOUR CREAM CINNAMON ROLLS

These unforgettable rolls were served at a Southridge pre-school board meeting on January 25, 1972, by Barbara Adams. Her friend, Joy Hesler, liked them so much she got the recipe and has used it many times since! For a sticky glaze, melt 1/4 cup margarine or butter, mix with brown sugar and place in bottom of the pan before putting in the rolls.

Filling
1 to 1 1/2 cups sugar
2 teaspoons cinnamon

1 (1/4-ounce) package dry yeast
1/4 cup warm water
1 cup sour cream
2 tablespoons shortening
3 tablespoons sugar
1/8 teaspoon soda
1 teaspoon salt
1 large egg, unbeaten
3 cups flour
1/4 cup melted butter

Combine sugar and cinnamon for filling and set aside. Dissolve yeast in warm water to proof. In a large saucepan heat sour cream to lukewarm. Add shortening, sugar, soda and salt. Stir until blended. Add egg and yeast; stir to mix. Mix in flour; knead until smooth. Cover with damp cloth and let rest 5 minutes. Divide dough in half. Roll to a rectangle about 14 inches wide and 1/4 inch thick. Spread with half of melted butter. Sprinkle with half of filling. Roll up jelly roll style and cut in 1 1/2-inch thick slices. Repeat with other half of dough. Place rolls in greased 9 x 13 pan. About 24 rolls will fit in pan, extra rolls can be put in a smaller pan. Let rolls rise about one hour. Bake 15 minutes at 375 degrees. After baking, remove from oven and invert immediately onto aluminum foil. Makes 24 to 30 rolls.

KEPT *ip: In making breads by hand, the first step is usually making sure the yeast is fresh and will help the bread to rise. You do this by mixing the yeast with lukewarm water and sometimes with a little sugar. In a few minutes, the dissolved yeast should form grayish, opaque bubbles—a good sign! If your yeast hasn't formed these bubbles, it hasn't "proofed," and you need to start again with fresh yeast.*

SUNFLOWER CLUB POTATO ROLLS

1 (1/4-ounce) package dry yeast
1/2 cup lukewarm water
1 cup hot milk
3/4 cup vegetable shortening
1 teaspoon salt
1/2 cup sugar
1 cup mashed potatoes
2 eggs, beaten
5 cups flour, divided

Dissolve yeast in lukewarm water to proof. Add shortening, salt and sugar to hot milk; mix well and cool until lukewarm. Add yeast, potatoes, eggs and 1 1/2 cups flour; mix well. Let rise until doubled in bulk, about 1 hour. Punch down and knead in remaining flour. Let rise again for one hour, then punch down. Roll the dough out to a thickness of 1/2 inch. Cut with round biscuit cutter. Place on lightly greased baking sheet. Bake at 425 degrees for 15 minutes or until golden brown. Makes 3 to 4 dozen rolls.

"My grandmother, Rhoda Brewer Marsh, was a member of The Sunflower Club, a group that met in Kansas City during the 1920s, 30s and 40s. Its members were women from Pittsburg, Kansas, who had moved to Kansas City. This recipe originated with the Sunflower Club. It's a family favorite.
Lynn Sample
Overland Park, Kansas

SANDY'S EASY CRESCENT ROLLS

Sandy Wheeler, Independence, Missouri, likes to bake ahead. This recipe, which is more than fifty years old, makes a dough that keeps in the refrigerator for several days "I love this recipe because it's so incredibly simple and the results are so delicious."

1 (1/4-ounce) package dry yeast
1/2 cup lukewarm water
3 eggs
1/2 teaspoon salt
1/2 cup sugar
1 cup melted butter, divided
1 cup warm milk
5 cups sifted flour

Dissolve yeast in warm water to proof. Beat eggs with salt and stir into yeast mixture along with sugar, 1/2 cup butter and milk. Place flour in large bowl and make a hole in the center. Pour liquid mixture into hole and mix thoroughly with a wooden spoon. Cover and refrigerate at least 4 hours or overnight. Cut dough into 4 sections and roll each section into a large circle. Spread with remaining 1/2 cup butter and cut into 8 wedges. Roll each wedge, beginning at the wide end, into a crescent shape. Cover and place in warm, draft-free place until doubled in size. Bake in 400 degree oven 10 minutes or until brown. Makes 32 rolls.

FRENCH BREAD

Elsie Albee of Sedalia, Missouri, makes this often. It's best when baked and served on same day.

1 (1/4-ounce) package dry yeast
1 1/2 cups lukewarm water, divided
2 tablespoons sugar
1 1/2 teaspoons salt
1 tablespoon vegetable shortening, at room temperature
4 cups sifted flour
1/4 cup butter, melted

Sprinkle yeast into 1/2 cup water, stir until dissolved. In a large bowl dissolve sugar and salt in remaining water. Add shortening and yeast mixture; mix well. Add flour, stir to mix well. Work dough with spoon at 10-minute intervals 5 times. Turn dough onto lightly floured surface; divide in half. Shape into 2 balls, let rest 10 minutes. Roll each ball into a 9 x 12-inch rectangle, then roll up firmly jelly-roll style; seal edge. Place loaves on cookie sheet. Score top. Bake 45 minutes to 1 hour, until golden brown. Brush top with butter.

TUSCAN BREAD

1 (1/4-ounce) package dry yeast
1/2 teaspoon sugar
2 cups lukewarm water
4 cups unbleached all-purpose flour
1/2 cup whole wheat flour
1/2 teaspoon salt
1 egg beaten with 1 teaspoon water, optional

Dissolve yeast and sugar in warm water to proof. Place unbleached flour, whole wheat flour and salt in bowl of food processor fitted with steel blade; mix well. With motor running, pour yeast mixture into processor; process until mixture forms a ball. Surface will be somewhat smooth and elastic but quite soft. If mixture doesn't form ball after 1 minute, add about 2 tablespoons flour. Turn out onto lightly floured board and knead until smooth. Add more flour if necessary to handle, but dough should remain somewhat sticky and moist. Form dough into a ball. Place in large, oiled bowl, and turn dough to oil top. Cover with towel or plastic wrap, and let stand in warm place until double, about 1 1/2 hours. Dust a baking sheet with flour. With floured hands, knead dough briefly in bowl to eliminate air bubbles. Cut into two equal pieces. Shape each piece into a 14-inch round loaf, and place several inches apart on prepared baking sheet. Cover with towel. Let rise in warm place 30 minutes. If desired for added browning, brush loaves with beaten egg mixture. Bake in 400 degree oven 40 minutes, or until bread is browned and loaves sound hollow when tapped on bottom. Cool on wire racks. Makes 2 loaves.

"The Tuscan bread recipe is a favorite because it's one of the few things I make that my daughter really likes. Also, it's easy and has a great texture, even when it doesn't rise as much as I expect."
Janet Majure
Lawrence, Kansas

CHALLAH

Kaleen Tiber, Kansas City, Missouri, makes many kinds of wonderful bread and this is one of the best. She says it also makes great toast and French toast.

1/4 cup plus 1 teaspoon sugar
1 cup warm water, divided
1 (1/4-ounce) package dry yeast
1/2 cup oil
2 teaspoons salt
2 large eggs
4 cups flour
1 egg yolk, beaten with 1 teaspoon water, for glaze
poppy or sesame seeds, for glaze

Rinse large mixing bowl with hot water and dissolve 1 teaspoon sugar in 1/2 cup warm water. Sprinkle yeast on top to proof. Stir in oil, water, 1/4 cup sugar, salt and eggs. Add half of the flour; mix well. Cover dough and let rise 2 hours. Add remaining flour; mix well. Knead on floured board until smooth and elastic. Place in greased bowl, turning to coat ball of dough. Cover and let rise until double, about 1 to 1 1/2 hours. Punch dough down. Divide into 3 equal pieces. Form each piece into a 14-inch strand. Pinch ends of strands together and braid into a loaf. Place in greased 9 x 5 loaf pan. Cover, let rise until double. Gently brush with egg yolk mixture and sprinkle with poppy seeds or sesame seeds. Bake at 375 degrees for 30 to 45 minutes. When done, bottom will sound hollow when tapped. Remove from pan, cool on wire rack. Makes 1 loaf.

KCPT*ip: For a delicious appetizer, thinly slice and toast the sourdough bread, then serve topped with thin slices of roasted beef tenderloin topped with a mixture of mayonnaise, sautéed mushrooms, bacon crumbles, and horseradish.*

GREEK ISLE BREAD

1/2 cup water
2 cups bread flour
3 tablespoons plain yogurt, not non-fat
2 teaspoons dry milk powder
1 tablespoon sugar
1 teaspoon salt
2 teaspoons butter
1/4 teaspoon garlic powder
4 teaspoons finely chopped black olives
1/2 teaspoon dried sweet basil
1/2 teaspoon dried dill weed
2 1/2 tablespoons feta cheese, drained well and
   crumbled
2 1/2 tablespoons peeled, seeded and puréed cucumber
1/2 teaspoon bread machine yeast

Put all ingredients into the bread pan in order listed. Follow machine directions to bake. Makes one 1 to 1 1/2-pound loaf.

ITALIAN SOURDOUGH BREAD

1 cup sourdough starter (from a packaged mix)
3/4 cup warm water
2 tablespoons olive oil
2 teaspoons salt
3 1/4 cups bread flour
2 1/4 teaspoons bread machine yeast

Place ingredients in bread machine pan in order given. Follow machine directions for a "rapid" cycle. The amount of bread flour may need to be adjusted, depending on the consistency of the sourdough starter. The dough should ball and just pull away from sides of pan during kneading. Makes one 1 to 1 1/2-pound loaf.

PRAIRIE SAGE CORNMEAL BREAD

Food writer and Overland Park, Kansas, resident Judith Fertig loves this version of cornbread. "The loaf comes out very light . . . and has a great taste," she says.

2 cups bread flour
1/2 cup yellow cornmeal
1 tablespoon fresh sage, minced fine
1/2 teaspoon salt
2 tablespoons honey
2 teaspoons butter
1 cup water
1 1/2 teaspoons bread machine yeast

Put all ingredients into the bread pan in order listed. Follow machine directions to bake. Makes one 1 1/2-pound loaf.

PARMESAN PEPPERCORN BREAD

Mary Caldwell, Kansas City, Missouri, loves baking bread in her bread machine. "I come home at lunch, put in the ingredients, and we have hot bread for dinner.

1 cup plus 2 tablespoons lukewarm water
1 tablespoon olive oil
3 1/4 cups bread flour
1/2 cup grated parmesan cheese
1 tablespoon sugar
1 teaspoon salt
3/4 teaspoon cracked black peppercorns
2 1/2 teaspoons bread machine yeast

Put all ingredients in the bread pan in the order listed. Follow machine directions to bake. Makes one 1 1/2-pound loaf.

Sweets

Kansas Citians love sweets! Our favorites? Anything chocolate and apple cake! Plus home-made cookies that have been passed from generation to generation, luscious pies that utilize the fruits of the Heart-land seasons, made-from-scratch cakes to celebrate a special event or a family dinner. These comfort foods get us through the roughest of days and provide a sweet ending to perfect evenings.

Blueberry Citrus Tarts

Buttermilk Pie

White Chocolate Raspberry Pie

Bess Truman's Lemon Ice Box Pie

Cranberry Apple Pie

Apple Upside-Down Cake

Fresh Apple and Black Walnut Cake

Prize-Winning Pumpkin Pie Cake

Kentucky Butter Cake

Sweet Chocolate Custard Cake

Mysterious Chocolate Torte
with Almond Creme

Glazed Fresh Apple Cookies

Sunflower Cookies

Swedish Oatmeal Cookies

Grandmother Amelia's Schmeerbaaken

Charles' Decadent Brownie Sundae

Hasty Pudding

Coconut Rum Flan with Starfruit

...and more!

BLUEBERRY CITRUS TARTS

1 cup (2 sticks) butter, at room temperature
3/4 cup sifted powdered sugar
2 cups flour
1 1/2 cups fresh blueberries
Powdered sugar, for garnish
Fresh orange zest curls, for garnish

Topping
4 eggs
1 1/2 cups sugar
1/3 cup lemon juice
2 tablespoons freshly grated lemon peel
1/4 cup flour
1 teaspoon baking powder

Preheat oven to 350 degrees. Lightly grease a 9 x 13-inch baking pan. In a mixing bowl cream butter and powdered sugar until smooth. Add flour and mix until well blended. Press mixture into baking pan and bake for 20 minutes until golden. For the topping, in a mixing bowl combine all topping ingredients and beat for 2 minutes. Sprinkle berries over cooked crust. Pour topping mixture over berries, arranging berries with a spoon. Bake for 30 to 35 minutes until light brown and set. Cool thoroughly in pan on wire rack. Cut into triangles or bars and sprinkle with powdered sugar just before serving. Garnish with orange curls. Makes 12 to 16 servings.

Laura O'Rourke and Betsy Titterington are the founding partners of The Culinary Center of Kansas City. The recipes they've developed are simple, elegant and always take advantage of the season's freshest produce.

MELANIE'S PEACH-BERRY COBBLER

"I receive rave reviews every time I serve this. It's a great summer dessert when it's peach-picking time."
Melanie Thompson
Kansas City, Missouri

7 ripe peaches
2 cups blueberries
2 teaspoons grated lemon rind
1 tablespoon fresh lemon juice
1/4 teaspoon almond extract
3/4 cup plus 5 tablespoons sugar
1 cup flour sifted
1 teaspoon baking powder
1/2 teaspoon salt
1 egg, unbeaten
5 tablespoons butter, melted
2 teaspoons cinnamon
1/2 teaspoon nutmeg

Preheat oven to 375 degrees. Coat a 9 x 13-inch baking dish with vegetable spray. Blanch peaches, peel, cut in wedges. Spread peaches in baking dish, top with blueberries. In a small bowl combine lemon rind, lemon juice, almond extract and 3 tablespoons sugar; sprinkle over fruit. In a mixing bowl sift together flour, 3/4 cup sugar, baking powder and salt. Add egg, mix with fork until coarsely blended; do not overblend. Sprinkle topping in a very thin layer over berries, leaving a few open areas. Drizzle butter over topping. Combine cinnamon, nutmeg and remaining sugar, sprinkle over topping. Bake in top 1/3 of oven for 15 minutes. Increase temperature to 400 degrees; bake 12 to 15 minutes more until lightly browned. Allow to set for 20 minutes. Serve with vanilla ice cream. Makes 12 to 16 servings.

THE BEST CHOCOLATE PIE EVER

1 cup sugar
4 tablespoons cocoa
2 tablespoons cornstarch
3 eggs, separated
1 cup milk
1 teaspoon vanilla
1 tablespoon butter
1 (9-inch) baked pie shell
6 tablespoons sugar
1 teaspoon lemon juice

Preheat oven to 350 degrees. In a saucepan mix sugar, cocoa, and cornstarch. Beat egg yolks and add to saucepan along with milk. Cook over medium heat until thick, stirring constantly. Cool briefly. Add vanilla and butter. Stir until butter melts. Pour into baked pie shell. In a mixing bowl beat egg whites until stiff but not dry; add sugar gradually; add lemon juice last. Spread over pie. Bake for 12 to 15 minutes, until meringue is browned. Makes 6 to 8 servings.

"My mother, Jean Bennett, was raised in Georgia. This recipe came from Geri, a beloved woman who cooked for the family 75 years ago. I guarantee this is the best chocolate pie that you've ever had."
Susan Bennett White
Kansas City, Missouri

WHITE CHOCOLATE RASPBERRY PIE

12 ounces white chocolate
1/2 cup whipping cream, heated
1/4 cup butter, at room temperature
2 cups fresh raspberries (or best-quality unsweetened frozen whole raspberries, thawed and drained)
1 (9-inch) baked pie shell

In a small pan melt white chocolate, stirring until smooth. Mix in hot cream and butter, stir until butter is melted. Spread about 3 tablespoons of the white chocolate mixture over the bottom of the pie crust. Spread raspberries evenly over this. Pour remaining filling over berries. Refrigerate at least 2 hours before serving. Makes 8 servings.

Alice Osborn of Savannah, Missouri, perfected this scrumptious combination of chocolate, raspberries and cream. It looks beautiful and tastes even better!

BUTTERMILK PIE

2 cups sugar
1/2 cup (1 stick) butter, at room temperature
3 eggs
3 tablespoons flour
1/4 teaspoon salt
1 cup buttermilk
1 (9-inch) unbaked pie crust
1/2 cup chopped pecans, toasted

Preheat oven to 300 degrees. In a large mixing bowl cream sugar and butter until smooth. Add the eggs, one at a time, beating well after each addition. Combine the flour and the salt; add gradually to the butter mixture, mixing well. Add buttermilk, beating until well blended. Pour into pie crust. Sprinkle toasted pecans over the top of the filling. Bake for 1 hour and 15 minutes or until the filling is set. Cool thoroughly; chill until serving. Makes 8 servings.

TROPICAL PIE

4 eggs, beaten
1 1/2 cups sugar
1 cup coconut
1/2 cup (1 stick) margarine, melted
1/4 cup orange juice
1 tablespoon water
1 (9-inch) unbaked pie crust

Preheat oven to 350 degrees. In a large bowl combine eggs, sugar, coconut, margarine, orange juice and water; stir until well blended. Pour into pie crust. Bake for 45 minutes. Cool thoroughly and chill until serving. Makes 6 to 8 servings.

BESS TRUMAN'S LEMON ICE BOX PIE

2 eggs, separated
1/3 cup fresh lemon juice
1 tablespoon lemon zest
1/2 cup sugar, divided
1 (9-inch) prepared graham cracker pie crust
1 cup whipping cream

In a small saucepan whisk egg yolks with lemon juice and zest until well blended. Whisk in 2 tablespoons sugar; blend well. Cook over low heat, whisking often, until the mixture thickens and turns opaque. Mixture is done when it coats the back of a spoon. Remove from heat and cool. In a small bowl beat egg whites with another 2 tablespoons of the sugar until stiff peaks form; set aside. In a separate bowl, whip cream with remaining sugar until stiff peaks form. Fold lemon mixture into whipped cream and blend well. Then fold the egg whites into the cream mixture and blend well. Pour into pie crust and freeze until firm, about 1 hour. Makes 6 to 8 servings.

When the Truman home in Independence was the summer White House, Bess Truman would invite her friends over for an afternoon of canasta and serve this dessert on the back porch.

GRANDMA GREEN'S PUMPKIN PIE

1 cup pumpkin
1 cup sugar
2 eggs
1 tablespoon butter, melted
1 tablespoon sorghum
1 teaspoon cinnamon
1/2 teaspoon allspice
1/2 teaspoon nutmeg
1 scant cup milk
Dash of salt
1 (9-inch) unbaked pie shell

Preheat oven to 375 degrees. In a large bowl combine all ingredients; beat well with mixer. Place in pie shell and bake at 375 degrees for 10 minutes. Reduce heat to 325 degrees and continue to bake for approximately 1 hour. Makes 6 to 8 servings.

Thanksgiving isn't complete without pumpkin pie. However, this recipe from Mary Greenblatt of Kearney, Missouri, is so good that it's in demand all year round.

CRANBERRY APPLE PIE

Louise Bird of Lenexa, Kansas, likes to make this tangy, tasty pie in the fall to take advantage of our area's bountiful apple crop. For a special presentation, try a lattice-top crust.

Pastry for double crust pie
3 large apples, peeled, cored and cut into 8 pieces
1 cup fresh cranberries, rinsed
1/2 cup raisins
1/2 cup plus 1 tablespoon sugar
1 tablespoon cornstarch
1/2 teaspoon cinnamon
1 egg, lightly beaten
1 tablespoon water

Preheat oven to 400 degrees. Place bottom pastry in 9-inch pie pan. In a large bowl combine 1/2 cup sugar, cornstarch and cinnamon. Toss fruits in mixture. Pour into pan. Fit top crust over filling, seal edges. Make slits in top crust to vent. In a small bowl mix egg with water. Brush lightly over top crust. Sprinkle remaining sugar on top. Bake for 20 minutes. Reduce heat to 300; bake for 30 minutes. Makes 6 to 8 servings.

LESLIE'S RHUBARB PIE

"When I lived in Denver I had a rhubarb patch so I learned to make a lot of dishes using fresh rhubarb. This pie is one of my favorites—the recipe came from my friend Leslie Jordan."
Fran Goetz
Kansas City, Missouri

6 cups rhubarb, in 1-inch pieces
1 1/2 to 2 cups sugar
1 1/2 tablespoons flour
2 egg yolks, beaten
2 tablespoons cold water
Pastry for 2 (two-crust) pies
1 egg white, beaten

Preheat oven to 400 degrees. Place rhubarb in a large bowl. Pour boiling water over to cover. Let stand for 15 minutes; drain well. In a large bowl mix sugar, flour, egg yolks, and water; mix well. Stir in rhubarb. Place bottom pastry in two 9-inch pie pans. Pour rhubarb filling into pie shells, fit top pastry over filling. Seal and crimp edges. Brush tops with egg white. Cut hole in center to vent; decorate with slits (don't cut slits all the way through). Bake for 30 minutes; reduce heat to 325 and continue to bake until done, 30 to 60 minutes. Makes two pies.

PECAN PIE

1/2 cup (1 stick) margarine, at room temperature
1 cup sugar
3 eggs, lightly beaten
1/2 cup dark corn syrup
1/4 cup light corn syrup
1/4 teaspoon salt
1 teaspoon vanilla
1 cup pecans, chopped
1 unbaked deep dish pie shell

Preheat oven to 375 degrees. In a mixing bowl cream margarine. Add sugar gradually and cream until light and fluffy. Add beaten eggs and mix well. Add syrups, salt, vanilla and pecans and mix well. Pour into pie shell. Bake on lower rack of oven for 40 to 50 minutes or until filling is firm. Makes 8 servings.

PAT-IN-THE-PAN PIE CRUST

1/2 cup (1 stick) margarine, melted
2 teaspoons sugar
1 cup flour

Preheat oven to 350 degrees. In a medium bowl combine margarine, sugar and flour. Mix well and place in 8-inch pie pan. Spread with thumbs to cover bottom and sides of pan. Bake for 15 minutes. Makes one bottom pie crust.

"You may use all dark corn syrup; I like using 1/4 cup light corn syrup. The pie is very good topped with a dollop of fresh whipped cream."
Nina Stearns Swanson Overland Park, Kansas

It's always a joy to find a better way to do something. This wonderfully easy pie crust recipe comes from Allene Meek of Kansas City, Missouri, who has made it for years.

APPLE UPSIDE-DOWN CAKE

1/3 cup firmly packed brown sugar
1/4 cup corn syrup
1 (20-ounce) can sliced apples, drained (or 2 1/2 cups peeled, sliced apples)
1 1/2 cups flour
1/4 teaspoon salt
1 teaspoon baking powder
1/4 cup margarine, at room temperature
3/4 cup sugar
1 egg
1 teaspoon vanilla
3/4 cup apple juice
1 teaspoon grated orange peel
1/4 cup chopped nuts, optional

Preheat oven to 350 degrees. Spray a 9 x 9 x 2-inch baking pan with non-stick cooking spray. In a small bowl combine brown sugar and corn syrup; spread in bottom of baking pan. Arrange apples over the sugar mixture; set aside. In a large bowl combine flour, salt and baking powder; set aside. In mixing bowl beat together margarine, sugar, egg and vanilla until smooth. Add flour mixture alternately with apple juice, beating well after each addition. Stir in orange peel and nuts. Pour batter over apples. Bake for 40 minutes or until wooden toothpick inserted into center comes out clean. Remove from oven and invert on serving tray. Makes 9 servings.

DORIS' EUROPEAN APPLE CAKE

1/2 cup vegetable shortening
1/2 cup sugar
1/2 cup brown sugar
1 egg
1 1/2 cups flour
1/2 teaspoon salt
1 teaspoon baking soda
1/4 teaspoon cloves
1 teaspoon cinnamon
1/4 teaspoon allspice
1 cup chopped dates
1 cup finely diced Jonathan apples
3/4 cup finely chopped nuts
1/2 cup cold coffee

"Chill this cake before serving; flavor improves! Don't frost—that would detract from the yummy flavor."
Doris M. Sanders
Kansas City, Missouri

Preheat oven to 325 degrees. Spray a 9 x 9-inch baking pan with non-stick cooking spray. In a mixing bowl cream shortening, sugar and brown sugar until smooth. Add egg, beating well to mix. In a separate bowl combine flour, salt, soda, cloves, cinnamon and allspice. Add to sugar mixture, mix until well blended Add dates, apples and nuts; stir to mix. Add coffee, stirring until well blended. Bake 1 hour. Makes 9 servings.

FRESH APPLE AND BLACK WALNUT CAKE

This makes a very moist cake which freezes well. Pat Duffy of Independence, Missouri, likes to serve it warm, topped with ice cream or whipped cream. It's also very good with cream cheese icing.

1/2 cup shortening
1 1/2 cups sugar
2 eggs
3 cups finely diced apples
1 1/2 cups flour
1/2 teaspoon salt
1 teaspoon cinnamon
1/2 teaspoon nutmeg
1 teaspoon soda
1/2 to 1 cup black walnuts, chopped

Preheat oven to 350 degrees. Grease and flour a 9 x 13-inch baking pan. In a mixing bowl cream together shortening and sugar. Add eggs, one at a time, beating well after each addition. Add apples, stir to mix well. In a separate bowl, combine flour, salt, cinnamon, nutmeg, soda and walnuts. Add gradually to sugar mixture, mixing at low speed. Dough will be very stiff. Spread dough in pan. Bake for 40 minutes. Makes 16 servings.

22221 QUICK CAKE

"I got this recipe from Teri Bavley whose family calls it Swedish Cake, but no one knows why. It's very good and moist, low in fat too."
Dee Barwick
Fairway, Kansas

2 cups flour
2 cups sugar
2 teaspoons baking soda
2 eggs
1 (20-ounce) can crushed unsweetened pineapple, undrained

Preheat oven to 350 degrees. Grease a 13 x 9-inch pan. In a large bowl stir together flour, sugar, and soda. Add eggs; mix well. Add pineapple, mix well and pour batter into pan. Bake for 35 to 40 minutes until lightly browned.

ORANGE CAKE

1/2 cup orange juice
1 1/2 cups sugar, divided
Rind of 1 orange
1 cup raisins
1 cup chopped walnuts
3/4 cup buttermilk
3/4 cup vegetable oil
1 teaspoon vanilla
3 eggs, beaten
2 1/2 cups flour
1 teaspoon baking soda
1/2 teaspoon salt

Preheat oven to 350 degrees. Grease and flour a bundt pan. In a small bowl combine orange juice and 1/2 cup sugar; set aside. Grind orange rind in food processor until pulverized; add raisins and chop. Transfer to a mixing bowl and add walnuts. Add buttermilk, oil, vanilla and eggs; beat thoroughly. In a large mixing bowl, combine flour, remaining sugar, baking soda and salt. Add liquid mixture and blend until flour is absorbed. Spoon into bundt pan. Bake for 45 minutes. Cool in pan for 10 minutes, then invert onto a cake plate. Spoon orange juice and sugar mix over cake. Makes 12 servings.

KCPT *ip: Virginia Barry of Blue Springs, Missouri, likes to use this Orange-Apricot Icing on angel food, carrot or yellow cake. Blend 2 ounces cream cheese, 3 tablespoons butter and 3 to 4 tablespoons orange juice concentrate. Mix in 6 to 8 large dried apricots, finely chopped. Gradually add 3 1/2 to 4 cups powdered sugar, mixing well after each addition.*

The intense flavor of this moist rich cake comes from using the orange rind in addition to orange juice. Kathryn Clark, Lawrence, Kansas, shares the recipe and suggests making it the day before you plan to serve.

KENTUCKY BUTTER CAKE

"This is a moist and flavorful cake that needs no frosting. Sprinkle with a little powdered sugar just before serving. It's great with a scoop of French vanilla ice cream!"
Shirley Biastock
Leavenworth, Kansas

3 cups flour
1 teaspoon baking powder
1/2 teaspoon baking soda
1 teaspoon salt
1 cup butter
2 cups sugar
4 eggs
1 cup buttermilk
2 teaspoons vanilla

Butter Sauce
1 cup sugar
1/4 cup water
1 stick butter
1 tablespoon vanilla

Preheat oven to 325 degrees. Lightly grease the bottom of a tube pan. Sift together flour, baking powder, baking soda and salt. In a mixing bowl cream butter and slowly add sugar, beating until smooth. Beat in eggs one at a time. Combine buttermilk and vanilla. Add the dry ingredients alternately with the buttermilk mixture; blend well after each addition. Pour batter into tube pan and bake 65 minutes. For butter sauce, in a small saucepan combine sugar, water and butter. Heat until butter melts. Stir in vanilla; heat but do not boil. When cake is done, invert onto serving plate; prick top with a fork and slowly pour hot butter sauce over the cake. Brush the sauce around the sides of the cake. Makes 12 servings.

MILE-HIGH CARROT CAKE

1 1/2 cups oil
2 cups sugar
1 teaspoon vanilla
4 eggs
3 cups plus 1 tablespoon flour
2 teaspoons baking powder
2 teaspoons baking soda
2 teaspoons cinnamon
1/2 teaspoon salt
3 cups grated carrots
1/2 cup chopped pecans
1 cup raisins

Frosting
1 (3-ounce) package cream cheese
2 tablespoons corn syrup
2 1/4 cups powdered sugar
2 teaspoons vanilla

Preheat oven to 350 degrees. Grease and flour a 9 x 13-inch baking pan. In a mixing bowl cream together oil, sugar, vanilla, and eggs. Sift together 3 cups flour, baking powder, baking soda, cinnamon and salt. Add dry ingredients to sugar mixture alternately with carrots, blend well after each addition. Toss raisins and nuts with remaining tablespoon of flour; add to batter and stir to mix. Pour into baking pan and bake for 1 1/2 hours. Cool in pan on wire rack. For frosting, combine all ingredients and mix well. Makes 16 to 18 servings.

KCPT *ip: Bonnie Jones adds 2 teaspoons of grated orange peel to cream cheese frosting for a different flavor.*

"The Page Turners, our book club, meets once a month. We read a variety of authors, and travel together to visit sites of our books. And we have dessert at every meeting. This is one of our favorites."
Darci Evans
Overland, Park, Kansas

PRIZE-WINNING PUMPKIN PIE CAKE

1 (32-ounce) can pumpkin
4 eggs, lightly beaten
1 (12-ounce) can evaporated milk
1 1/2 cups sugar
2 teaspoons cinnamon
1 teaspoon nutmeg
1/3 teaspoon ginger
1 yellow cake mix
3/4 cup margarine, melted
1/2 cup chopped nuts

Preheat oven to 300 degrees. Lightly grease a 9 x 13-inch baking pan. In a large bowl combine pumpkin, eggs, milk, sugar, cinnamon, nutmeg and ginger; beat to mix well. Pour into baking pan. Sprinkle dry cake mix evenly over batter. Drizzle melted margarine over cake mix and sprinkle nuts on top. Bake for 1 hour and 20 minutes or until knife inserted in center comes out clean. Serve topped with whipped cream. Makes 16 servings.

CHOCOLATE CUPCAKES

2 cups sugar
1/2 cup vegetable oil
1/2 cup cocoa
2 eggs
1/2 cup sour cream
2 cups flour
1 1/2 teaspoons baking soda
2 teaspoons vanilla
1 cup hot water

Preheat oven to 325 degrees. Line muffin tin with paper baking cups. In a mixing bowl beat together sugar, oil and cocoa until smooth. Add eggs, mixing well. Add sour cream, flour and soda, beating to mix well. Add vanilla and hot water. Batter will be runny. Fill paper baking cups half full. Bake 20 to 25 minutes or until toothpick inserted in middle comes out clean. Makes 24 cupcakes.

MYSTERIOUS CHOCOLATE TORTE WITH ALMOND CREME

5 egg whites
1/8 teaspoon cream of tartar
1 teaspoon vanilla extract
1/8 teaspoon salt
1/2 cup sugar
1/2 cup flour
1/3 cup cocoa
Sliced almonds, for garnish

Almond Crème
1 cup sugar
3/4 cup water
1 teaspoon vanilla
1 cup condensed skim milk
1/4 cup almond liqueur

Preheat the oven to 350 degrees. Lightly oil a 9-inch springform pan. In a mixing bowl beat egg whites with cream of tartar, vanilla and salt until the egg whites begin to form stiff peaks. In a small bowl combine the sugar, flour and cocoa. Add the dry ingredients to the egg mixture 1/2 cup at a time, blending at low speed. Pour the batter into the springform pan and bake for 15 minutes. The cake may appear underdone, but do not leave it in the oven. Let cake cook in pan. For almond creme, in a heavy saucepan combine sugar, water and vanilla. Stir over medium heat until mixture turns a light brown, about 15 to 20 minutes. Remove from heat. Whisk in the condensed milk, then stir in liqueur. Sauce will keep covered in refrigerator for up to two weeks. When cake is cool cut into wedges and drizzle with the almond creme. Top with almond slices. Makes 6 to 8 servings.

"How can such a delicious choco-latey cake be low fat? It's a mystery! The low fat creme sauce is also good on pound cake, ice cream or fresh fruit. Substitute framboise or any favorite liqueur for the almond if you wish."
Judith Fertig
Overland Park, Kansas

SWEET CHOCOLATE CUSTARD CAKE

Who can resist a chocolate cake with chocolate filling? Not many people— especially when it's as delectable as this one from Bennie Blankenship of Warrensburg, Missouri. The recipe may sound like it contains a lot of steps, but it is worth every one. Try it once and you'll be addicted!

3 eggs, divided
1 1/2 cups milk, divided
1 2/3 cups sugar, divided
1 (4-ounce) bar sweet baking chocolate
1/2 cup (1 stick) butter, at room temperature
2 1/4 cups sifted flour
1 teaspoon baking soda
1/2 teaspoon salt
1 teaspoon vanilla

Sweet Chocolate Filling
1/4 cup milk
1/4 cup sugar
1 egg
1 (4-ounce) bar sweet baking chocolate
1/3 cup softened butter
2 1/2 cups powdered sugar
1 teaspoon vanilla
1 cup chopped black walnuts or pecans

Preheat oven to 350 degrees. Grease and flour three 8-inch round layer pans. In a small saucepan beat one egg and combine with 1/2 cup milk and 2/3 cup sugar; cook and stir over medium heat for about 2 minutes. Add chocolate, reduce heat to low and cook until chocolate is melted and mixture thickens; cool to room temperature.

In a mixing bowl cream butter and gradually add remaining cup of sugar; cream until light and fluffy. Add remaining eggs, one at a time; beat well after each addition. Sift flour with baking soda and salt. In a small bowl combine remaining milk and vanilla. Add flour mixture and milk alternately to the sugar and butter mixture, beginning and ending with the flour and beating well after each addition. Stir in cooled chocolate mixture until well blended. Pour evenly into the prepared pans. Bake for 25 to 30 minutes. Remove layers from pans to cool on wire rack.

For filling, in a saucepan combine milk, sugar and egg; mix well. Cook over low heat until mixture is thickened, stirring constantly. Remove from heat. Break chocolate into small pieces and add to hot mixture along with the butter, stirring until chocolate is melted. Beat until smooth and creamy. Blend in powdered sugar and vanilla. Add nuts and mix well. If filling seems too thick, stir in a small amount of milk. Spread filling between layers and on top. Makes 12 to 16 servings.

CHOCOLATE LOVER'S CAKE

2 cups sugar
2 cups flour
1/2 cup (1 stick) margarine
1/2 cup oil
4 tablespoons cocoa
1 cup water
2 eggs, beaten
1/2 cup buttermilk
1 teaspoon soda
1 teaspoon vanilla

Frosting
1/2 cup (1 stick) margarine
4 tablespoons cocoa
6 tablespoons buttermilk
1 (16-ounce) box powdered sugar
1 teaspoon vanilla

"This is a delicious moist cake. I especially like it because it is baked, frosted and served in the same pan."
Virginia Groseclose
Gladstone,
Missouri

Preheat oven to 350 degrees. Grease a 12 x 16-inch baking pan. Sift the sugar and flour into a large bowl. In a saucepan combine the margarine, oil, cocoa and water. Heat until margarine is melted. Pour over the sugar and flour; mix at low speed until blended. Add eggs, buttermilk, soda and vanilla; continue to mix until well blended. Pour into pan; bake for about 40 minutes. For frosting, in a saucepan combine margarine, cocoa and buttermilk. Bring to a boil. Add powdered sugar, a little at a time, until mixture is of desired consistency. Add vanilla, stir to mix well. Makes 16 servings.

CHOCOLATE RASPBERRY BROWNIE CAKE

1/2 cup (1 stick) butter or margarine
3 ounces unsweetened chocolate
1 1/3 cups sugar
1/2 cup chopped pecans or walnuts
2 eggs
1 teaspoon vanilla
2/3 cup all-purpose flour
2 1/2 cups raspberries, rinsed and dried
Powdered sugar

Preheat oven to 350 degrees. Butter and flour a 9-inch spring-form pan. In a large pan over low heat, stir butter and chocolate just until melted, about 5 minutes. Remove from heat and beat in granulated sugar, pecans, eggs and vanilla. Add flour and stir to mix well. Spread batter in springform pan. Next to the rim, spread 1 cup of the raspberries in a band about 2 inches wide; gently press fruit into batter. Bake 45 to 50 minutes or until the top, at outside edges, cracks and feels firm to touch. Let cool in pan on a rack. Remove rim and set cake on a plate; dust with powdered sugar, and mound remaining berries in the center. Makes 12 servings.

RASPBERRY SAUCE

1/2 cup orange juice
1/4 cup granulated sugar
1 tablespoon cornstarch
1 (10-ounce) package frozen raspberries

In a saucepan combine orange juice, sugar and cornstarch; whisk together until smooth. Add frozen raspberries. Cook over high heat, stirring constantly, until mixture comes to a boil. Reduce heat and simmer for 5 minutes, or until mixture thickens, stirring constantly. Serve warm or transfer to container; cover and refrigerate. May be used cold or gently warmed. Makes approximately 2 cups.

GLAZED FRESH APPLE COOKIES

1 1/3 cups brown sugar
1/2 cup shortening
1 egg
2 cups flour
1 teaspoon baking soda
1 teaspoon cinnamon
1/4 teaspoon salt
1/4 cup apple juice or cider
1 1/2 cups chopped, peeled apple
1 cup chopped nuts
1 cup raisins
1/4 teaspoon cloves

Glaze
1 1/2 cups powdered sugar
2 tablespoons milk
1 tablespoon butter
1/4 teaspoon vanilla

Preheat oven to 400 degrees. In a mixing bowl cream sugar and shortening until smooth. Add egg, beat until fluffy. In a separate bowl combine flour, soda, cinnamon and salt. Add to sugar mixture and beat at low speed until just blended. Add apple juice, mix well. Add apples, nuts, raisins and cloves, stir to mix. Drop by tablespoonfuls onto a greased cookie sheet. Bake 7 to 8 minutes. Remove to wire rack to cool. For glaze, in a small bowl combine sugar, milk, butter and vanilla; beat until creamy. Glaze cookies while still warm. Makes 3 dozen cookies.

"I got this recipe from a church friend 12 years ago and have made it many times since then. It's a favorite with both children and adults."
Arlene Benham
Shawnee, Kansas

SUNFLOWER COOKIES

1 cup vegetable shortening
1 cup sugar
1 cup brown sugar
2 eggs
1 teaspoon vanilla
1 3/4 cup flour
1/2 teaspoon baking powder
1 teaspoon baking soda
1/4 teaspoon salt
2 cups quick-cooking oats
1 cup flaked coconut
1 cup sunflower seeds

Preheat oven to 350 degrees. In a mixing bowl cream shortening, sugar, and brown sugar until light and fluffy. Blend in eggs and vanilla. Sift together flour, baking powder, soda, and salt; add to sugar mixture; beat at low speed until just blended. Stir in oats, coconut, and sunflower seeds. Drop by spoonfuls onto ungreased cookie sheet. Bake for 8 to 10 minutes or until brown. Cool on wire rack. Makes 3 dozen cookies.

KCPT*ip: This recipe for Quick No-Bake Peanut Butter Cookies comes from Louise Bird of Lenexa, Kansas. In a medium saucepan combine 2 cups sugar, 1/4 cup cocoa and 1/2 cup water. Bring to a rolling boil and cook for 1 minute. Remove from heat and mix in 1/2 cup peanut butter. Add 3 cups uncooked oatmeal and mix well. Drop by teaspoons on waxed paper. Work quickly for they set up fast. Makes 1 1/2 dozen cookies.*

CAPE COD OATMEAL COOKIES

1 1/2 cups whole wheat flour
1/2 teaspoon baking soda
1/2 teaspoon salt
1 1/2 teaspoons cinnamon
1/4 cup (1/2 stick) butter, melted
1/2 cup canola oil
1/2 cup dark brown sugar
1 egg
1 tablespoon sorghum molasses
1/4 cup soy milk
1 3/4 cups uncooked rolled oats
3/4 cup raisins
3/4 cup chopped English walnuts

Preheat oven to 350 degrees. In a large bowl mix flour, baking soda, salt and cinnamon. In a separate bowl cream butter, oil, sugar, egg, molasses and soy milk until smooth. Add flour mixture, beat at low speed until just blended. Add oatmeal, stir to mix. Add raisins and walnuts, stir to mix. Drop by teaspoonfuls on a non-stick cookie sheet. Bake for 10 to 15 minutes, until slightly firm to the touch. Cool on wire rack. Makes about 2 dozen cookies.

Sandra Leigh Custard of Kansas City, Missouri, is a great cook and her cookie-making skills are legendary. Friends especially like these flavorful oatmeal cookies.

MERINGUE MINT KISSES

2 egg whites
Pinch of salt
1/2 teaspoon cream of tartar
3/4 cup sugar
1/2 teaspoon vanilla
Mint flavoring
3 to 4 drops green food coloring
1 (6-ounce) package chocolate chips

Preheat oven to 350 degrees. In a mixing bowl, beat egg whites, salt and cream of tartar until stiff. Slowly add sugar; beat until glossy. Add vanilla, flavoring, food coloring, and chocolate chips, stir to mix. Drop by teaspoonfuls onto greased cookie sheets. Turn oven off. Place cookies in oven; leave overnight. Store cookies in air-tight container. Makes 4 dozen cookies.

LEMON TEATIME COOKIES

1 cup (2 sticks) butter
1/3 cup powdered sugar, sifted
3/4 cup cornstarch
1 1/4 cups flour
1/2 cup finely chopped pecans

Frosting
1 cup powdered sugar, sifted
1 teaspoon butter
2 tablespoons lemon juice

Preheat oven to 350 degrees. In a mixing bowl cream butter and sugar until light and fluffy. Add cornstarch and flour; beat at low speed until just blended. Chill dough until easy to handle. Shape into 1-inch balls. Scatter nuts on waxed paper or foil and place balls of dough on top. Flatten with the bottom of a tumbler dipped in flour. Using a spatula, place cookies on ungreased cookie sheet, nut side down. Bake for 12 to 15 minutes. Cool on wire rack. For frosting, in a mixing bowl cream sugar, butter and lemon juice until smooth. Frost when cool. Makes 2 1/2 dozen cookies.

PUMPKIN COOKIES

2 cups flour
1 cup sugar
2 teaspoons baking powder
1/2 teaspoon baking soda
1/4 teaspoon nutmeg
1 teaspoon cinnamon
1 egg
3/4 cup vegetable oil
1 cup canned pumpkin
1 teaspoon vanilla
1 (6-ounce) package semi-sweet chocolate chips

Preheat oven to 350 degrees. In a large bowl combine flour, sugar, baking powder, soda, nutmeg and cinnamon; mix well. In a separate bowl, beat together egg, oil, pumpkin, and vanilla. Add dry ingredients, beating until just blended. Stir in chips. Bake for 15 to 20 minutes. Makes 3 dozen cookies.

Randy Withrow of Overland Park, Kansas, especially likes to make these spicy cookies in the fall. Great for lunchbox treats.

POTATO CHIP COOKIES

1 cup white sugar
1 cup brown sugar
1 cup shortening
1 teaspoon vanilla
2 eggs
2 cups flour
1/4 teaspoon salt
2 teaspoon soda
1 cup crumbled potato chips
1 cup chopped nuts

Preheat oven to 350 degrees. In a mixing bowl cream sugar, brown sugar, shortening, and vanilla until smooth. Add eggs one at a time, beating after each addition. In a separate bowl combine flour, salt and soda. Add gradually to sugar mixture, beating at until just blended. Stir in chips and nuts. Bake 10 to 12 minutes. Cookies will be soft when done, but will harden after removing from oven. Makes 3 dozen cookies.

No, these cookies don't taste like potato chips, but they do taste very good! Mary Conrad of Kansas City, Kansas shared this unusual recipe.

SWEDISH OATMEAL COOKIES

When she was growing up in Sweden, Barbro Lucas of Fairway, Kansas, learned to make these cookies from her mother, Margareta Andersson. Barbro added the almond flavoring. So good and so easy!

1 cup (2 sticks) butter (no substitution)
1/2 cup sugar
1/2 teaspoon almond flavoring, optional
1 cup flour
2 cups oatmeal

Preheat oven to 350 degrees. In a mixing bowl cream butter, sugar, and almond flavoring if desired. Add flour and oatmeal, beating at low speed until just blended. Shape dough into 1-inch balls, place on ungreased baking sheet and flatten slightly with a fork. Bake for 10 to 12 minutes, until light brown. Makes 3 dozen cookies.

GRANDMA'S ICE BOX COOKIES

"This is the cookie I most remember having as a child. During World War II, this was the cookie mother sent to the boys in the service who wrote that even the crumbs were good!"
Selma Dreiseszun
Kansas City, Missouri

1 cup sugar
1 cup brown sugar
1 cup shortening
3 1/2 cups flour
2 teaspoons cinnamon
1 teaspoon baking powder
1 teaspoon baking soda
3 eggs
1 cup chopped nuts

In a mixing bowl cream sugar, brown sugar and shortening until smooth. Add eggs, beating to mix well. In a separate bowl combine flour, cinnamon, baking powder and baking soda. Add to sugar mixture, beating at low speed until just blended. Add nuts, stir to mix. Shape dough into 4 rolls, each about 2 inches in diameter. Roll in wax paper and refrigerate several hours. (The dough keeps well in the refrigerator; you can slice and bake as needed.) When ready to bake preheat oven to 350 degrees. Cut dough into 1/8-inch slices. Place on ungreased cookie sheet and bake for 10 to 12 minutes. Makes 8 dozen cookies.

SANTA'S WHISKERS

1 cup (2 sticks) butter at room temperature
1 cup sugar
1 tablespoon milk
1 teaspoon vanilla or 1/2 teaspoon rum extract
2 1/2 cups flour
3/4 cup finely chopped red or green candied cherries
1/2 cup finely chopped pecans
3/4 cup flaked coconut

In a large mixing bowl, cream butter and sugar until fluffy. Add milk and vanilla; beat well. Add flour and beat until well mixed. Stir in cherries and pecans. Divide into thirds. Shape each portion into a 7-inch long roll. Roll each in 1/4 cup of the coconut to coat. Wrap in foil and chill for several hours. When ready to bake preheat oven to 375 degrees. Cut dough into 1/4-inch slices. Bake for 10 to 12 minutes or until edges are lightly browned. Makes 6 dozen cookies.

"Ever since I first made these, my wife has insisted that it's just not a proper holiday without Santa's Whiskers! Cutting the cookies off the roll is easier with a wire cheese slicer."
R. Douglas Reed
Kansas City, Missouri

KOLACHI

1 (3-ounce) package cream cheese
1/2 cup (1 stick) unsalted butter
1 cup sifted flour
1 teaspoon vanilla or almond extract
1 teaspoon cinnamon, optional
Jam, any flavor desired
1/2 cup powdered sugar

In a food processor combine all ingredients. Process until just blended. Remove and form into a round. Wrap and chill 30 minutes. Preheat oven to 375 degrees. Cut dough into quarters; rewrap three quarters and return to refrigerator. Roll out the other on floured board, to about 1/8-inch thick. Cut with a 2-inch cutter. Place a spoonful of jam on each; fold sides over jam and press together. Crimp edges to seal. Bake for 15 minutes. Remove from oven and toss in powdered sugar. Makes 2 dozen cookies.

"The filling for these cookies can really be anything you want. I've used dried fruit, chocolate chips and nuts. Adjust the extract to fit filling . . . almond with date or vanilla with chocolate chips."
Barbara Davis
Olathe, Kansas

GRANDMOTHER AMELIA'S SCHMEERBAAKEN

"My grandmother made these cookies in the shape of a 3-inch long figure eight, and my family thinks that's the only shape that 'tastes right.' This recipe has been in our family for generations."
Suzanne G. Locher
Shawnee Mission, Kansas

2 cups (4 sticks) butter, at room temperature
2 cups sugar
2 eggs
1 cup ground almonds
4 1/2 cups flour

Preheat oven to 400 degrees. In a mixing bowl cream butter, sugar and eggs until light and fluffy. Add the ground almonds and mix well. Add 4 1/2 cups flour gradually, beating at low speed until just blended. Press dough through a cookie press fitted with desired shapes onto an ungreased cookie sheet. Bake 8 to 10 minutes or until the edges are lightly browned. Cool on wire racks. Makes 6 to 8 dozen cookies.

DOROTHY'S CHRISTMAS COOKIES

"My mother used to make these lovely, soft sugar cookies at Christmas time. She got the recipe from the Kitchen-Klatter radio show out of Shenandoah, Iowa. As a child I hated that show. But now I've come to appreciate the recipes."
Joy Winter
Kansas City, Kansas

3 cups sifted flour
2 teaspoons baking powder
1 scant teaspoon baking soda
1/2 teaspoon nutmeg
1/2 cup vegetable shortening
1/2 cup (1 stick) butter
2 large eggs
1 cup sugar
4 tablespoons sweetened condensed milk
1 teaspoon vanilla

In a large bowl combine flour, baking powder, soda and nutmeg. Cut in shortening and butter. In a mixing bowl beat eggs; add sugar, milk and vanilla. Beat well. Pour into flour mixture; beat until blended. Chill dough until firm. When ready to bake, preheat oven to 375 degrees. Roll 1/4 of the dough at a time on floured board, to about 1/8-inch thick. Cut into shapes and bake for 8 to 10 minutes or until lightly browned. Makes 3 dozen cookies.

ALMOND COOKIES

1 1/2 cups (3 sticks) butter, at room temperature
1 cup white sugar
3/4 cup brown sugar
3 eggs, lightly beaten
4 1/2 cups sifted flour
1 teaspoon salt
1 teaspoon baking soda
1 tablespoon cinnamon
1 cup sliced almonds.

In mixing bowl cream butter and sugar until smooth. Add eggs, beating until well blended. In a separate bowl mix flour, salt, baking soda and cinnamon. Add gradually to sugar mixture, blending at low speed. Stir in nuts. Shape dough into 4 rolls, each 2 inches in diameter. Wrap in wax paper and freeze until firm. When ready to bake, preheat oven to 375 degrees. Cut cookies into 1/8-inch slices. Bake on greased cookie sheet for 10 to 15 minutes. Makes 6 to 8 dozen cookies.

CHOCOLATE FUDGE COOKIES

1 1/2 cups chocolate chips
2 tablespoons butter or margarine
1 (14-ounce) can sweetened condensed milk
1 cup flour
1 cup chopped walnuts

Preheat oven to 325 degrees. In a saucepan melt chocolate and butter. Remove from heat and stir in remaining ingredients. Drop by teaspoonfuls on an ungreased cookie sheet. Bake for 8 to 10 minutes. Cookies should be firm, but are over-done if a crust forms on top. Cool on wire rack. Makes 2 dozen cookies.

"This is my grandmother's recipe. My father fondly remembers 'sampling' these cookies which were stored in glass jars in his closet before Christmas. Apparently my grandmother didn't notice that the volume of cookies steadily diminished!"
Joyce Kemp
Mission Hills, Kansas

"These cookies are a chocolate lover's dream! And very easy to make. They are pretty when frosted with a simple chocolate icing (canned will do) and topped with pecan halves."
Alice Osborn
Savannah, Missouri

KATIE'S MINT BROWNIES

This recipe for an absolutely luscious treat comes from Katie Oyler, Raytown, Missouri. "Be sure not to cut these brownies in too-large squares," she warns. "They are very rich."

1 cup (2 sticks) margarine, melted
2 cups sugar
2 tablespoons vanilla
4 eggs
1 cup flour
2/3 cup cocoa
1/2 teaspoon baking powder
1/2 teaspoon salt

Mint layer
2 cups powdered sugar
2 tablespoons crème de menthe
1/2 cup margarine

Glaze
1 (6-ounce) package semi-sweet chocolate chips
6 tablespoons margarine

Preheat oven to 350 degrees. Lightly grease a 9 x 13-inch baking pan. For brownie, in a mixing bowl cream margarine, sugar and vanilla until smooth. Add eggs, mix well. In a separate bowl combine flour, cocoa, baking powder and salt. Add gradually to sugar mixture, blending at low speed. Pour into baking pan. Bake for 20 to 25 minutes or until brownie begins to pull away from the edges of the pan. Place pan in freezer to cool. For the mint layer, in a mixing bowl cream powdered sugar, crème de menthe and margarine until smooth. Spread over cooled brownie. Return brownie to freezer. For the glaze, in a saucepan combine chocolate chips and margarine. Stir over low heat until melted. Cool slightly then spread evenly over mint layer. Chill and cut into squares. Makes 16 servings.

CHARLES' DECADENT BROWNIE SUNDAE

1 1/4 cups sugar
1/2 cup (1 stick) butter, at room temperature
2 eggs
3 1/2 cups hot fudge sauce, divided
1 1/2 teaspoons vanilla extract
1 1/3 cups flour
1/4 teaspoon baking soda
1/4 teaspoon salt
1/2 cup chopped nuts, optional
1/2 gallon frozen custard or vanilla ice cream, for
  topping

Preheat oven to 350 degrees. Grease a 9 x 13-inch baking pan. In a mixing bowl beat together sugar, butter, eggs, 1 1/2 cups of the hot fudge sauce and vanilla until smooth. In a separate bowl combine flour, soda and salt. Add gradually to sugar mixture, stirring to mix. Stir in nuts, if desired. Spread batter in baking pan. Bake for 20 minutes or until a wooden pick inserted in the center comes out slightly sticky. Cool in the pan. Cut into 12 squares. To make the sundaes, place each brownie in a serving dish. Top with a scoop of custard or ice cream and drizzle with remaining hot fudge sauce. Makes 12 sundaes.

Man-about-town, food critic and newspaper columnist Charles Ferruza, Kansas City, Missouri, is usually too busy to cook, but when he does, he creates something fabulous like this delightful dessert.

JILL'S COCONUT RUM FLAN WITH STARFRUIT

*"I'm a flan fanatic!
I love it! This
recipe is one I
developed through
much trial and
error. It's based on
a recipe from
Steven Raichlen.
My Brazilian
friends call it
'pudim' and
request it at every
potluck and party."*
Jill Silva
Kansas City,
Missouri

Caramel Sauce
1 cup sugar
1/4 cup water

Custard
1 1/2 cups canned coconut milk (available in Asian
    groceries or some large supermarkets)
1 (14-ounce) can sweetened condensed milk
5 eggs, lightly beaten
3 tablespoons rum
2 teaspoons vanilla
1 teaspoon cinnamon
1/2 teaspoon nutmeg
1 quart boiling water
Starfruit, sliced, for garnish

Preheat oven to 350 degrees. For caramel sauce, in a small saucepan combine sugar and water. Cover pan and cook over high heat 2 to 3 minutes. Remove cover. Cook 3 to 4 more minutes, until caramelized to a golden brown. (Watch carefully as it burns easily.) Pour hot caramel in the bottom of an 8-inch round baking dish or individual ramekins. Swirl mixture to distribute evenly over the surface. Do not touch caramel as it is very hot! For custard, in a large mixing bowl whisk together coconut milk, condensed milk, eggs, rum, vanilla, cinnamon and nutmeg. Pour mixture through a mesh strainer into caramel-lined dish. Carefully place dish in the bottom of a roasting pan. Pour boiling water in roasting pan to 1-inch depth, creating a water bath. Place pan in oven and bake 40 to 50 minutes, or until a toothpick inserted in center of custard comes out clean. (If using individual ramekins, begin checking at 30 minutes.) Remove from oven, cool to room temperature, then refrigerate at least 6 hours before serving. To serve, slide a knife around the edges of flan, place a serving plate over top and invert quickly. Place starfruit slices over top for garnish. Makes 8 servings.

CREAM PUFF CAKE

1 cup water
1/2 cup (1 stick) butter, no substitution
1 cup flour
4 eggs
3 (3-ounce) packages instant vanilla pudding
1 (8-ounce) package cream cheese, at room temperature
4 cups milk
1 (12-ounce) tub non-dairy topping

Preheat oven to 400 degrees. Grease a 9 x 13-inch baking pan. To make crust, in large saucepan bring water and butter to boil. Add flour, stirring until ball forms. Remove from heat. Add eggs, one at a time, beating well after each addition. Spread mixture in baking pan. Bake for 30 to 35 minutes, until golden brown. Cool. For filling, in a mixing bowl blend pudding, cream cheese and milk until smooth. Pour over cooled crust. Cover with topping. Keep refrigerated until ready to serve. Makes 16 servings.

Cindy Barton of Independence, Missouri, makes this unusual dessert for special occasions. It is very reminiscent of the cream puffs grandma used to make. Drizzle chocolate or strawberry syrup over top, if desired.

HASTY PUDDING—90'S STYLE

1/4 cup cornstarch
1/3 cup sugar
2 cups milk, divided
1 egg, beaten
1 teaspoon vanilla
2 tablespoons butter or margarine

In a 2-quart microwave bowl, combine cornstarch and sugar; mix thoroughly. Add 1/2 cup of the milk and mix to form a smooth paste. Add the rest of milk; stir to blend. Microwave for 6 minutes, 1 1/2 minutes at a time, stirring after each interval. The pudding base should be beginning to thicken nicely. Add a small amount of base to the egg. Mix thoroughly, then return the egg mixture to base and blend to an even texture. Microwave 2 minutes, in 30-second intervals, stirring after each interval. Add vanilla and butter; stir to mix until butter is melted. Refrigerate until cooled. Makes 4 servings.

"Homemade pudding is one of my all-time favorite comfort foods and this is a recipe I concocted to take a lot of the work out of making it. For chocolate pudding add 3 tablespoons cocoa to the cornstarch and sugar." Kayla Folger Topeka, Kansas

MARK'S FAVORITE BREAD PUDDING WITH SAUCE

"I first tasted bread pudding in New Orleans. I loved it and developed my own version, which makes a very dense, rich pudding."
Mark Ronfeldt
Shawnee Mission, Kansas

1/2 cup (1 stick) butter
2 cups milk
16 cups cubed, day-old French bread
1 cup pineapple chunks
1 cup raisins
1 cup sugar
1/2 teaspoon salt
1 teaspoon cinnamon
1 teaspoon nutmeg
4 eggs, beaten
2 teaspoons vanilla

Sauce
1/2 cup (1 stick) butter, at room temperature
4 cups powdered sugar
1/2 cup of your favorite libation—whiskey, coffee, brandy, flavored liqueur (milk or cream may also be used)

Preheat oven to 350 degrees. Butter a 9 x 13-inch baking dish. In a saucepan combine butter and milk, heat until butter is melted. In a large mixing bowl combine bread, pineapple and raisins. Pour milk mixture over bread mixture. Stir to mix well and let stand until bread absorbs liquid. In a separate bowl combine sugar, salt, cinnamon and nutmeg. Add eggs and vanilla; mix well. Pour over bread mixture and place in baking dish. Bake for 40 to 50 minutes or until toothpick inserted into center comes out clean. For sauce, in mixing bowl cream together butter and powdered sugar until smooth. Slowly add liquid; beat until smooth. Serve pudding warm with sauce. Makes 16 servings.

KCPT *ip: For pudding with a creamier texture, bake in water bath. Bread pudding is a versatile dessert. Experiment with your favorites—substitute diced apples for pineapple, finely chopped dried apricots or prunes for raisins.*

COOKS OF "THIS PLACE CALLED HOME"

Barbara Adams
Colleen Adams
Karen Adler
Elsie Allee
Mellody R. Allee
Virginia M. Barry
Cindy Barton
Dee Barwick
Stephanie Barwick
Teri Bavley
Carol Belt
Arlene Benham
Jane Berkowitz
Shirley Biastock
Louise Bird
Bennie Blankenship
Bev Boney
Debby Burkhardt
Nancy Caldwell
Mary Carroll
Peter Castillo
Kathryn G. Clark
Dee Conde
Mary Conrad
Mrs. "Coop" Cooper
Frank Cooper
Terry Cooper
Sharon Cottitta
Carole Cottrill
Sarah Crooks
Sandra Leigh Custard
Rhesa Dane
Ardie Davis
Barbara Davis

Rich Davis
Cheryl Dennis
Luella Dick
Rita Downey
Ruby Downing
Selma Dreiseszun
Mary Ann Duckers
Pat Duffy
Darci Evans
Sandra Famuliner
Charles Ferruza
Judith Fertig
Kayla Folger
Tina Fontenot
Joseph M. Gaccamo
Jan Girando
Debbie Globoke
Fran Goetz
Lisa Waterman Gray
Mary Greenblatt
Virginia Groseclose
C.W. Gusewelle
Jane Guthrie
Dee Harding
Kristin Hatch
Barnett Helzberg, Jr
Joy Hesler
Bill Hickok
Linda Hill
Dianne Hogerty
Susan Hornung
Maxine N. Howard
Bill Hunt
Lois Hunt

Joyce Ann Jaillite
Gary Jensen
Ellen Johnson
Bonnie Jones
Judith Bader Jones
Rose Kallas
Keitha Kaminsky
Joyce Kemp
Shirin Khodayari
Roselyn Kraack
Millie Krna
Georgia Kuehn
Carol Kuse
Beverly Lang
Mary Pfeifer Langley
Louis Lauth
June Lewallen
Bonnie Livingston
Mary Loberg
Suzanne G. Locher
Herb Long
Barbro Lucas
Lee Major
Lindsay Major
Janet Majure
Warren Maus
Terressa McGee
Allene Meek
Sharon Mellor
Karen Merry
John and Laura Mertz
Beverly Mettlen
Kathryn Moore
Sara and Bill Morgan

Marty Morris
Claire Northamer
Laura O'Rourke
Diane O'Byrne
Bill and Sharon Orr
Alice Osborn
JoAnne Owens
Pam Owens
Katie Oyler
Carlene Pasche
Betty Payne
Lucylle Perry
Leigh Peterman
Marci Pickard
Anthony Pickert
Pat Poretta
Jennifer Prusa
Barbara Reed
Mary Ann Reed
R. Douglas Reed
Sarah Huntman Reed

Karen Regan
Lois Riemath
Wanda Riordan
Jan Rodgers
Joseph J. Roh
Mark Ronfeldt
Lynn Sample
Doris M. Sanders
Barbara Scanlon
Ed Scanlon
Penny Seavertson
Jill Silva
Cort Sinnes
Pauline Van Slyke
Andrea Smith
Kathy Howell Smith
Shifra Stein
Melanie Stevens
Nina Stearns Swanson
Nancy Swanwick
Lou Jane Temple

Melanie Thompson
Kaleen Tiber
Betsy Titterington
Evelyn Toner
Kay Tucker
Mariann Herndon
Vandenberg
Barbara Wacker
Jane Wagner
Judi Walker
Sally Wallace
Lesley Wallingford
Sandy Wheeler
Susan Bennett White
Jill Winn
Bonnie Winston
Joy Winter
Randy Withrow
Pat Wright
Roxanne Wyss
Peggy Zilm

INDEX OF RECIPES

ORDER FORM

Order Direct!

Kansas City customers call 756-3580 x4244

Faxes also welcome: (816) 751-6272

To order by email: cookbook@kcpt.org

Please rush the following to me:

_____ copy(s) **This Place Called Home, a Kansas City Cookbook**
@ $17.95 per copy plus $4.00 Shipping and Handling

Method of Payment

_____ Enclosed is my check for $_____ payable to KCPT

Please charge to Visa_____ MC_____ Discover_____ Amex_____

Card Number _____

Expiration Date _____

Name _____

Address_____

City_____State_____Zip _____

Ship to: (if different than above)

Name _____

Address_____

City_____State_____Zip _____

Mail completed form to:
KCPT – Channel 19, 125 E. 31st
Kansas City, MO 64108
Attn: Cookbook